More than

MANCHESTER
UNIVERSITY PRESS

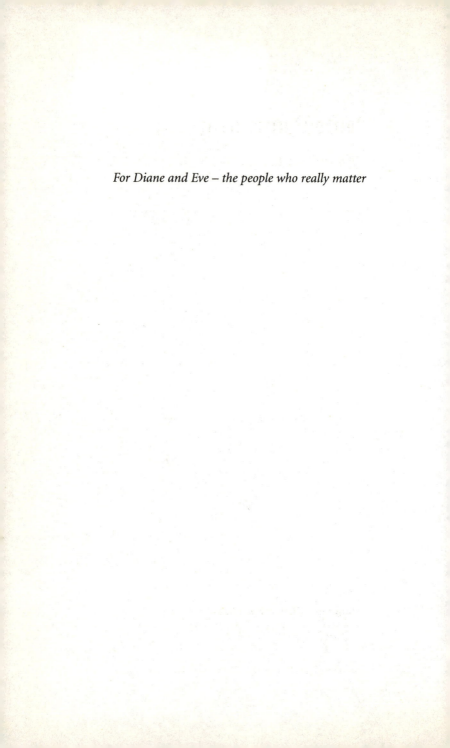

For Diane and Eve – the people who really matter

More than a game

The computer game as fictional form

Barry Atkins

Manchester University Press

Manchester and New York

distributed exclusively in the USA by Palgrave

Published by Manchester University Press
Oxford Road, Manchester M13 9NR, UK
and Room 400, 175 Fifth Avenue, New York, NY 10010, USA
www.manchesteruniversitypress.co.uk

Distributed exclusively in the USA by
Palgrave, 175 Fifth Avenue, New York, NY 10010, USA

Distributed exclusively in Canada by
UBC Press, University of British Columbia, 2029 West Mall,
Vancouver, BC, Canada V6T 1Z2

British Library Cataloguing-in-Publication Data
A catalogue record for this book is available from the British Library

Library of Congress Cataloging-in-Publication Data applied for

ISBN   0 7190 6364 7 *hardback*
         0 7190 6365 5 *paperback*

First published 2003

11 10 09 08 07 06 05 04 03   10 9 8 7 6 5 4 3 2 1

Typeset by Freelance Publishing Services, Brinscall, Lancs
www.freelancepublishingservices.co.uk
Printed in Great Britain
by Bell and Bain Ltd, Glasgow

Contents

Acknowledgements

Thanks go to my colleagues in the Department of English, Manchester Metropolitan University. Margaret Beetham and Jeff Walsh encouraged me to pursue this project when I had doubts, and Michael Bradshaw and Kate McGowan were perfect colleagues during the period of writing. I would also like to acknowledge the support offered by the department's Research Committee, who gave me time to think by granting me study leave at a crucial time. I am not sure that this is the project I described on my application, but I hope they are not too disappointed. Erikka Askeland, Diane Atkins, Jo Smith and Robert Elliott read sections in progress. Simon Malpas read the whole thing, despite my neglect of the fantasy roleplaying games that so fascinate him. While he is no way to blame for the wilder excesses of this study, or even for the bits in between, his advice and conversation were essential to its growth and development. I would also like to thank the anonymous technician who performed minor miracles to connect my PlayStation to the university audio visual equipment the first time I rashly decided to give an academic paper on this material. I have no more credits.

1 The computer game as fictional form

For when the One Great Scorer comes
To write against your name,
He marks – not that you won or lost –
But how you played the game.
                    (Grantland Rice)

Life's too short to play chess. (H. J. Byron)

The origins of this project can be located in an experience that could not have been further distanced, at the time, from the academic practice and teaching of cultural and literary criticism which usually fills my days: the successful conclusion of *Close Combat II: A Bridge Too Far* (1997), a strategic wargame set in the Second World War. In addition to the usual feelings of unease at the amount of potentially productive research time that I had spent in solitary 'communication' with the intriguingly named, and necessarily limited, 'artificial intelligence' that was produced at the intersection between the game's designers and my even then lowly Pentium 166 MHz processor, I had a growing feeling of disquiet at what I had been engaged in as the final clip of film rolled. Black and white archive footage of a ceremony at which bearded and exhausted *Wehrmacht* soldiers received decorations in the field was accompanied with a stentorian voice-over delivered in a thick Hollywood-German accent. Apparently, my leadership qualities had earned me the personal thanks of Berlin. In destroying the bridgehead at Arnhem, and stalling the Allied armoured advance well before it reached Nijmegen, I had been responsible, potentially, for altering the course of the war in the West. Bully for me.

The intrusion of language into the world of the game had pulled me up short. Intellectually capable as I was of divorcing the abstract gameplay and pixelated graphics that had eaten into my spare time over a number of weeks from any notion of a 'real' Second World War, a 'real' parachute assault on Arnhem, and a 'real' Adolf Hitler, winning not just the game, but the approval of even a simulation of Nazi Germany left me feeling a little flat, to say the least. I was also well aware that if I mentioned my military triumph in the English department where I am a lecturer, then I might find myself treated with the kind of suspicion usually reserved for those who appear to have mistaken the military history section of the bookshop for the top shelf of a newsagents as they browse hard-back illustrated volumes with titles like *Uniforms of the Waffen-SS, 1939–45*, or *Camouflage Schemes of Operation Desert Storm*. Playing games with virtual toy soldiers and rewriting the history of the Second World War to the advantage of Nazi Germany was nothing to be proud of.

And yet there was something here that was as intriguing as it was disturbing. A game that was marketed through a rhetoric of 'authenticity', as 'realistic' and a 'simulation', had led to a substantially inauthentic deviation from its ostensible historical referent. In layman's terms, somewhere in the interaction between myself and the game a fictional version of a historical military campaign had been created. That I had largely been led by the nose through a series of extremely restricted episodes representing small-scale military conflicts in order to construct this narrative did not interest me so much as the process of construction itself. Perhaps there were the first signs here of a form of fiction that I had not been aware of before, the creation of a new type of 'text' that required critical reading in a way that differed from the critical reading of novels, films or television texts? As an increasingly popular form of fiction that made grand claims for authenticity and realism in its marketing, and presented a type of what I thought I recognised as storytelling outside language, the computer game certainly seemed to demand further consideration.

At the risk of indulging in the sort of pretentiousness that sees academics making an occasional unwelcome appearance in *Private Eye* magazine's 'Pseuds Corner', it also seemed that I had encountered something that might have at least tenuous connections with what has come to be termed 'counterfactual' history and has seen popular expression in novels such as Philip K. Dick's *The Man in the High Castle* (1965) or, more recently, Robert Harris's *Fatherland* (1993). I had, in my own limited and solitary way, been as much engaged in the exploration of the historical 'what if?' as any of the contributors to Niall Ferguson's edited collection of essays, *Virtual History: Alternatives and Counterfactuals* (1998). There was a tension inherent in this form of game between historical truth claim and fictional possibility. Its counterfactual potential might have been severely limited (the Allied defeat at 'the bridge too far' at Arnhem is a historically verifiable event, as well as a successful film) but it was nevertheless present (the extent of that defeat was nothing like the game experience). The extent of the deviation from the report of historical event, apparently, had been my responsibility. Fiction and history appeared to be caught in a complex relationship that needed teasing out.

Computer wargames such as the *Close Combat* series display a near-obsession with questions of historical authenticity and realism. In terms of the details of weapons performance, unit deployment, and terrain modelled on period aerial reconnaissance photographs, *Close Combat* seeks to attain a level of detail that would satisfy the most retentive of military history's trainspotters. In a phrase discussed further in Chapter 4, the manual for one game in the series declares that it 'puts the emphasis on real' within the genre of 'real-time strategy' games. Yet it was something that had emerged out of a lack of correspondence with real event that is inherent in this kind of game that had most disturbed me (the variant narrative that I had constructed, or at least been complicit in constructing), and notions of fiction-making that had most interested me.

The initial feelings of disquiet remained, however. The very abstraction of the game's structure, and its status as (just a) game, provided a defence against some of the most obvious forms of criticism that such a fiction might encounter. This was the kind of 'clean' representation of warfare of which Brussels and Washington can only dream. No Dutch citizens are caught in crossfire or risk reprisals – this German war-machine is the product of programming information and not of an economy dependent on slave labour. The politics of the story are just not an issue. The armchair general faced with a computer did not have to concern himself or herself with questions of right or wrong, or separate the good guys from the bad guys. It all depended, quite literally, on your 'point of view'. In this text the human tragedy and drama of the Second World War, and even the human evil of Nazi militarism, had no relevance – all that was offered were a series of equations and apparent facts free from the implied moral judgements of storytelling as I moved the mouse and tapped the keyboard.

I was reminded of Ernest Hemingway's famous and oft-quoted statement on the consequences of the experience of modern warfare in *A Farewell to Arms* (1929):

> [there] were many words that you could not stand to hear and finally only the names of places had dignity. Certain numbers were the same way and certain dates and these with the names of places were all you could say and have them mean anything. Abstract words such as glory, honor, courage, or hallow were obscene beside the concrete names of villages, the numbers of roads, the names of rivers, the numbers of regiments and the dates.[1]

What *Close Combat* seemed to provide was a version of post-Hemingway recounting of war, albeit one with which even such a believer in the beneficial nature of sports and games with clearly defined rules might well have had little sympathy. Hemingway's narrator is seeking escape from the betrayal of a particular kind of narrative, that of propaganda: the player of *Close Combat* was freed from received historical recounting. Until that final voice-over, he or she was released, even, from the kind of judgements inherent in the construction of story through language. An elimination of connective narrative accounting (the links between isolated 'facts' that give story its meaning) left only those isolated and apparently objective fragments of data which, like the sidebars of historical information to be found within the printed manuals for *Close Combat*, provided a fractured version of the past uncluttered by political, economic, social and (most particularly) human context. On the level of the individual story episode the player was provided with the building blocks of a story that was then 'written' or 'told' through its playing out according to the internal logic of the game. Here was a form of fictional freedom: I could tell the story again and again and bring the story to a variety of conclusions. Here was a form of fictional restraint: I could only tell the story in a particular way. There really was something here that demanded further thought.

That the computer game has not, to date, received much serious critical attention as an independent form of fictional expression, rather than in passing as a technological curiosity or as a springboard for some extremely speculative theorising about the possibilities that might one day be revealed in virtual reality or cyberspace is hardly surprising, however. If this is a form of fiction, then it is still perceived as a form of fiction for children and adolescents, with all the pejorative associations that such a classification carries with it. Games, with their vast time demands and lack of discernible product in their near-onanistic engagement of an individual with a machine, have hardly been welcomed with open arms by the parents of their target audience. 'Adult', when it is invoked as a term at all, most often equates with 'pornographic', rather than 'sophisticated'.

That some of the same criticisms made of computer games might be levelled at the practice of reading more traditional texts (no clear product, time taken up that might be better used running around in the open air, the generation of what appears to be obsession in genre fictions like J. R. R. Tolkien's *The Lord of the Rings* (1954–55)) does not seem to have broken down the basic antipathy towards the *game* element of the computer game. Reading has 'value', even the reading of the most popular forms of genre fiction: the playing of games 'wastes time' that might have been put to better use.

If one were to push a comparison between the computer game and literature further, then the concentration of game designers and consumers on genres that are fairly low down the literary pecking order (war, science fiction, fantasy) does little to add to the respectability of the computer game. But it might be as short-sighted to ignore questions of how we 'read' computer texts, and how they communicate their meanings, particularly in this time of increasing computer 'edutainment', online education, electronic publishing, and increasing Internet use, as it would be to ignore questions of just how we read other forms of popular text.

Looking along the CD rack beside my computer led me to a series of further digressions that would eventually take in the serious consideration of games belonging to a range of what appear at first to be very different sub-genres. Games as superficially diverse as 'first-person shooters', 'third-person adventures' and those management games often referred to as 'god games' appeared to be creating fiction in new ways just as much as the real-time strategy game *Close Combat*. What connected many of the games I had played, however, was the way in which they claimed varieties of 'realism'. If the computer game is another form of fiction, as I have come to believe and argue throughout this volume, then it is different in more than mere technicalities of form from film, television, or prose fiction. The stories we read in computer games are not just pale reflections of novels, plays, films, or television programmes, but they have a different relationship with both other textual forms and the 'real world' that it (and other forms of 'realist' fiction) claim to represent. As telling a story on the written page has different demands, constraints and freedoms, as well as conventions of representation, than the telling of a story on the stage, or on film, or on television, so the telling of stories within computer games works with different conventions that are not solely located in its foundation on the basic binary operation of the computer's processor. The technology deployed in the service of the computer game is important, and requires due attention, but it is at least as important to pay close attention to the ways in which games designers and players have exploited the strengths and weaknesses of the modern computer as a vehicle for the delivery of fictional texts.

The computer game's claims to authenticity and realism, whether in terms of historical simulation and the accuracy of its data arrays, the 'real physics engines' of flight and road simulations, the advances in graphics that now see mirrored reflections off surface water and deep shadows cast by flickering light sources, or the complex algorithms that lie underneath the often jolly graphics of management games such as the *Civilization* or *SimCity* series, all seem to demand a particular kind of investigation. The fundamental differences between these various forms of computer game also need identification if we are to comprehend their varying intersections and engagements with the terms 'realistic' and 'simulation' that so often appear on their packaging.

The invitation to a particular individual and even unique form of 'reading' that such games offer within a reader–text interaction that is qualitatively removed from that offered by other visual or written forms similarly requires examination. If we accept that we are confronted with a form of narrative storytelling where the production of story is the end result of play, as well as with a game where 'winning' is everything, then analysis of those storytelling processes becomes necessary. As a primarily literary critic, with some background in academic historiography (the study of how history is written), this new mode of computer-based storytelling seems to me to be both amenable to contemporary literary-critical practice, and related practices deployed within cultural studies, and to demand a somewhat different critical approach. The formal characteristics of this as an independent form need examination if the computer game is to be treated with the seriousness, as a massively popular form of cultural expression, that it deserves. To simply condemn or ignore this developing form of fiction as 'childish', rather than recognise its 'immaturity', might well be a mistake. This study offers suggestions, through example, of a practice of reading computer games that in no way constitutes a rigid methodology, but might be among the first faltering steps towards such a critical undertaking. I make no apology for the concentration on questions of narrative practice that may appear to be fairly old news for those who are familiar with contemporary critical theory as it has been read in relation to literature and film. Such areas as I attempt to cover in detail, including narrative 'point of view', the possibility of 'subversive readings', 'closure', the meaning of terms such as 'realism', 'counterfactual historiography' and the handling of time within narrative are in no way original to me – the originality of the intervention I intend to make is in my consideration of these terms and ideas when we look at specific works in detail, rather than fall into the trap of writing in vague and general terms about the computer game in the abstract.

The postmodern temptation

Plenty of writers of more or less unreadable critical and theoretical works have claimed that their books are intended for that mythical beast 'the general reader', and I am not keen to join their company. I have, therefore, attempted to keep the amount of theoretical jargon (rather than serious thought) to a minimum. Nor am I alone in my scepticism towards some of the more extreme language that can be used when this new technology is up for discussion. As Jon Covey has argued in his introduction to *Fractal Dreams*, 'Each onslaught of hyperactive technobabble becomes more tedious than the last, until we become just plain bored.'[2] I would not even attempt to glorify my own argument – it is intended to be introductory, preliminary, and to raise questions as to where we go next as critics and readers, as much as it is intended to provide comprehensive answers about the past, present, or future of the computer game. The endnotes are there for those who want them, although not to any length or extent that would protect this work from possible charges of being overly reductive in aiming for clarity of argument over fullness of scholarly reference. The computer game-fiction is a form of popular fiction and I, like many other critics who work in the hinterland of what goes under the name of cultural studies, would argue that scholarly rigour is as essential in approaching such popular texts (and I use Roland Barthes' term 'text' self-consciously, just as I have insisted on the italicisation of their titles as if they have equal standing with films or novels) as it is when approaching the supposedly high-cultural textual artefact. This present work, however, is primarily intended as introductory in tone and content – I do not want to bury my arguments for what is new, distinct, or different in this form of popular entertainment too far under a language or methodology that is undeniably popular in academia, but is rarely accessible, understood, or even particularly popular beyond its confines. I seek to inform, but not to validate my arguments through either jargonistic 'technobabble' or philosophical musings that are not firmly anchored in observation.

That said, I freely admit that I have drawn far more on theories of narratological analysis (and to give an early example of the kind of simplifying gloss I will be guilty of throughout this study, I would define narratology for my purposes here as the study of how stories are told) than on poststructuralist or even postmodern thought.[3] My ambition is relatively limited – the games I isolate as my examples, I contend, require informed reading as fiction and as texts. They deserve, and get in this study, no more and no less. To give an early indication of where I hope to have travelled to by the end of this study, my provisional answer to the question of whether the computer game is 'more than a game' is a qualified 'yes' – it can also be a form of fiction making, and in the cases I isolate presents a fictional text that rewards close critical scrutiny. Is it 'more than a game' in that it requires a reformulation of our understanding of self, identity, art, or culture? Is it representative of a truly radical break with the ways in which we have previously told ourselves our stories? 'No', or at least 'No, not yet.'

This is a form of self-denial and self-restraint, and not always of ignorance. This is not intended to be a work of theoretical enquiry, but a work of close textual criticism. In concentrating on specific game-fictions *as* fictions, and looking in detail at concrete examples of the form, I try to avoid making too many hyperbolic claims, and to restrict myself to that which can be supported by readings sourced in the texts themselves. Specifically, I have recognised in myself a tendency to make too much of an apparent correspondence between the texts I have been reading 'through' or 'on' my PC and PlayStation, and those I have been reading that exist within works of contemporary critical theory. What I have termed the 'postmodern temptation' in this section heading is something I have sought to both recognise and deny, partly to keep this study manageable, and partly to try and avoid moving too far into abstraction and generalisation. In particular, I have tried to avoid 'applying' theory to texts, and using the tricks and tropes of rhetorical argument to patch over the resulting gaps and absences.

Before I completely alienate a possible academic readership, however, I would like to make it clear that this is not an antitheoretical move. What I want to suggest is that it is far too tempting for the academic critic to consider the future possibility of what the computer game might become, rather than address the mundanity of the object we actually have access to. This is not that potentially oxymoronic thing, an 'untheorised reading'. Rather, it is a reading that draws on narratological and structuralist thinking and criticism for the most part, and tries to leave its more speculative digressions until the closing chapter. Those who wish to read about *Tomb Raider*, *Half-Life*, *Close Combat*, or *SimCity* are advised to skip ahead to the beginning of Chapter 2 and read on. Those who wish to see if I have anything new to say about the future possibility of the computer game might be best advised to endure this section of the text and then skip ahead to Chapter 6. Much of the (hopefully unobtrusive) theoretical material that follows and informs this study emerged out of enquiries into supposedly 'simple' or 'primitive' narrative forms such as the fairy tale or folk tale, and seems to have particular utility in the examination of the computer game if we recognise its own 'primitive' or 'simple' current state. What theoretical material there is that talks to and about intimately related cultural phenomena such as 'virtual reality', however, is concerned with a far more complex and sophisticated object of study. Jean Baudrillard's essay 'Aesthetic Illusion and Virtual Reality', discussed in Chapter 6, for example, would seem to be as astute and as forcefully argued as much of his other work, but not to be straightforwardly applicable to the world of 'left click this', 'hit that shortcut key' and 'save the game'.[4]

The very materiality of the experience of playing the computer game, its engagement with bits of plastic and metal, silicon and glass, fix it still within the age of mechanical reproduction that was identified by Walter Benjamin even as there is a potentially digital or even 'cyber' age evolving or revolving about it.[5] Things might be about to change, but the reality of playing computer games at the turn of the twenty-first century requires a mass of cables and plugs and extensions. Wires snake about everywhere. Get too involved in playing and your back will ache, your eyes will suffer strain and your mouse hand will begin to cramp. The computer game takes its toll on the body even as it promises a disembodied and virtual experience. Next time we feel inclined to chuckle about our digital forebears and find it amusing that huge mechanical monsters used to occupy the computer departments of our universities, we should take a long hard look at the cables and peripherals that trail across the floor of our living rooms or underneath our desks and computer stands. The machine remains a physical presence, and a bulky one at that. And if we should ever feel the urge to stress just how primitive it was to shove stacks of cards punched with holes into early computers then we might reflect on what we are doing as we drop another disk into the CD drive of our PC or console. Our more elegant contemporary machines, our i-Macs and laptops, might not be the physical mess of your average PC setup at the turn of the twenty-first century, but they remain bulky reminders of the physical (and not virtual) nature of the phenomenon.

The language that surrounds the computer game (terms such as 'game' and 'play') and the language that surrounds other emergent forms of computer-dependent text (such as 'hypertext' and 'simulation'), offers an almost overwhelming temptation to its early critics, who appear – like me – to be faced with something that seems to emerge out of that particular period that Fredric Jameson has termed 'late capitalism', and Jean Baudrillard has characterised as 'the "proteinic" era of networks ... the narcissistic and protean era of connections, contact, contiguity, feedback and generalized interface that goes with the universe of communication', and to already share a basic terminological vocabulary with much postmodern thinking.[6] As such it is tempting to point either an admonitory or celebratory finger at computer games and declare them to be somehow symptomatic or representative of the postmodern. Those who would see the postmodern as a moment (an extended cultural event, a period), rather than a practice or loose collection of practices, might be forgiven for making immediate connections between this moment and a cultural product that so firmly belongs to it. The formulation is simple, if not simplistic. Now is postmodern. The game-fiction did not exist before now. The game-fiction is therefore postmodern. QED. Or, to use the language of the early arcade video games, 'Game Over'.

Leaving aside any evaluation of the utility of making such a critical move for a moment – that does little more than slap a dated label on the side of the game-fiction and remind us that it is undeniably contemporary – it is nevertheless worth spending a little time tracing some of the more subtle connections that can be made, and that I have nevertheless avoided drawing on too heavily in the case of the individual textual studies examined here. We should always remember Jameson's own characterisation of the postmodern as a site of contestation rather than critical or definitive certainty, but several early interventions in the debates that have surrounded the postmodern are worth examining briefly here.[7] The postmodern theorist Ihab Hassan's oppositional list of binary categories, for example, might have been received with understandable scepticism, and be open to criticism for its portrayal of a clearly defined modernism and a clearly defined postmodernism drawn up in battle lines rather than in intersection and debate, but it still offers some potential illumination as to why it is so tempting to see the computer game as being locatable within postmodern theoretical frameworks:

Modernism	*Postmodernism*
purpose	play
design	chance
centering	dispersal
genre/boundary	text/inter-text
interpretation/reading	against interpretation/misreading
lisable (readerly)	*scriptable* (writerly)
origin/cause	difference–*différance*/trace[8]

Were we to accept such a pair of lists without the usual pinch of salt we might think that the computer game might be firmly placed in the postmodern camp, and might even be representative, to follow Hassan's more complex argument in *The Dismemberment of Orpheus*, of a postmodern fictional form of representation that can truly be termed 'anti-elitist' (essentially popular, democratic, even demotic), rather than 'elitist' (text always fixed within hierarchies of value and reference) in a fashion that has proved problematic within literary criticism. To begin with the obvious, and in recognition that the compound term game-fiction I deploy throughout this volume incorporates rather than rejects the *game* element within *game*-fiction, it is certainly a case of 'play' over 'purpose', as so much of the negative criticism levelled at the computer game has made clear.[9] Less certainly there is the presentation of chance over design – as the game reproduces the effect of 'chance' (the availability of plural possibility) over 'design' (the inevitability of a singular outcome, some kind of fixed and 'authored' outcome). Similarly, we see in that plurality of possibility a 'dispersal' rather than a 'centering,' and at least the illusion of the *scriptable* (writable, privileging the reader) over the *lisable* (readable, privileging the author).[10] What we would lose if we succumb too readily to such critical temptations, however, would be this need for a specificity of analysis. As enough literary critics have found, if we are not careful in our definitions we are in danger of finding 'the postmodern' in every time and place, in the history plays of Shakespeare, and in the very first novels in English. I sometimes wonder what we might make of the prehistoric cave art of Lascaux if we always carry our postmodern critical apparatus with us when we confront an artwork.

Having been subject to intense theoretical debate since the 1970s, terms such as 'simulation' and 'hypertext' also press obvious critical buttons. In the terms of common usage (at least with regard to the textual organisation of the World Wide Web, both within specific pages and between websites), 'hypertext' offers non-linear and non-hierarchical communicating linkages between textual fragments, but it is not simply a technological enactment of what Gérard Genette is concerned with when he discusses 'hypertextuality'.[11] Context might well be boundless, but we would do well to remember its specificity. As Jean Baudrillard has noted when discussing 'simulation' in a wider social and cultural context it is possible to argue that 'simulation threatens the difference between 'true' and 'false,' between 'real' and 'imaginary'.[12] As such it seems to offer an attractive point of access for thinking through the computer game – particularly for those who might foresee a technological future in which we might 'lose ourselves' in the 'consensual hallucination' of the 'matrix' of cyberspace.[13] We should, however, continue to be careful in our use and understanding of such terms, never coined and rarely subject to critical reassessment in the face of the encounter with the computer game. As the actual experience of reading computer games should remind us, such terminology does not always survive its transportation to the specifics of that experience. I would ask the reader to pause and insert the words 'computer game' before Baudrillard's statement. Is 'true' and 'false', 'real' and 'imaginary' really 'under threat' in such games?

It is worth pointing out here that the 'sim' of *SimCity* is truncated and partial for a reason – 'simulation' in computer games is not the same as the kinds of 'simulation' that necessarily pose any such 'threat'. In the games themselves, rather than the hyperbolic copy written by their promotional teams, they rarely support any claim to threaten this distinction in any meaningful way. In Chapter 3 I argue in detail that if the first-person computer game is simulating something, then it is certainly not simulating lived experience. It might, however, be useful in explaining my reticence towards 'using' postmodern thought if we quickly look here at some of the ways in which we can draw a distinction between Baudrillardian 'simulation' and the forms of 'simulation' one actually encounters within the computer game as it currently stands. In *Gunman Chronicles* (2000), for example, we encounter a comparatively advanced visual experience that uses the same graphics engine as *Half-Life*. It is presented from a first-person point of view that allows us to pretend that we are 'in' this environment. *Gunman Chronicles* is a three-dimensional text, in which we use a combination of mouse and keyboard to move about this 'virtual' world. Largely we move about in order to reposition the gunsight that allows us the crude form of interaction (shooting things) that is central to the playing of the game, but we are also provided with an illusion of freedom of visual movement. Playing for a while, however, indicates that there is a hierarchy of effective 'simulation' in the game. The artificiality of topography and architecture are barely noticeable as we become accustomed to what amounts to the visual 'style' of the game. There are too many angles and bright colours for this to be convincing in its illusory potential, but not in a way that intrudes too much on our reading experience. Water does not look like 'real' water, but is recognisable as water in terms of negative definition. It has enough markers of the characteristics of water (it moves, it reflects, it is semi-transparent) that we recognise it as not earth, not corridor, or not lava.

But the human figures of the other gunmen that move and shoot and run about this landscape are recognisably not human. We might be fooled for a moment that they looked 'as if' they were human, that there was ever an 'original' (as there is in the traditional filmed image before it is manipulated in the studios of Industrial Light and Magic), but not for long. Glimpsed for an instant in the distance we might not bring our knowledge of their graphic limitations to mind. But close up, they look remarkably inhuman – there is little individuation, they 'pose' like bodybuilders at rest rather than stand naturally, and they are square-jawed not because they are action heroes, but because the framework of graphical boxes (or polygons) from which the image is composed is still evident on the most superficial level. The games designers have built in some nice touches, and these figures twitch and fidget with small random movements rather than stand stock-still, for example, but there is absolutely no way that anyone could mistake the computer-generated image for an apparent image of the real such as film. When the figures speak then the lack of effective lip-synching reminds us of just how primitive this is if it is understood to be an attempt at 'simulation'.

Computer-animated films that have attempted this feat of presenting an image with no original as if there was an original, such as *Shrek* (2001), *Monsters Inc* (2002) or *Final Fantasy* (2001) are interesting enough as technical demonstrations of what happens visually when millions of hairs are modelled individually, or how the potential of each successive advance in computer processing power is harnessed to give apparent texture to skin, but in their attempt at the representation of the human always suffer comparative failure. Who could not have noticed, for example, that Princess Fiona in *Shrek* is far more 'convincing' a figure when she is in ogre form than when she is her 'human' self? Or that the toys of *Toy Story* 'convince' in a way that the humans do not? Ogres, or the walking eyeball of *Monsters Inc*, or the hardware of a science fiction future in *Final Fantasy*, are comparatively convincing in their 'illusion' that the image presented could have been connected mechanically with a 'real' object because that 'real' object is actually located within the imagination (and our tradition of representation of the imagination) and not in the observed world. This is far harder to achieve digitally when it is poor flawed humanity that is the subject of representation. And I am sure those actors who provide the voices so essential to the success of such films will be laughing all the way to the bank when they read of the imminent redundancy of the human because of technological advance.

It is telling that where a game like *Gunman Chronicles* succeeds visually is in its rendering of images that have no meaningfully real reference – at the top of its hierarchy of 'simulation' is not the human or the inanimate, but the dinosaurs that populate the first alien landscape that the player encounters. Of course, when we test the representation of the human in the computer game for its 'accuracy' or its 'realism' we make comparison with the observed real as well as with other acts of representation – when we test the 'accuracy' or 'realism' of the dinosaurs we test against a tradition of representation. These are not lizards with bits glued on, as we once encountered in the monster movies. Nor is this the stop-motion animation of models, as in films where animators such as Ray Harryhausen stunned audiences with the realism of the reptiles, such as *One Million Years B.C.* (1966). What it refers to is the current 'state of the art' and not the state of the real. *Jurassic Park* (1993) showed the way, and (at least in the UK) BBC television's *Walking With Dinosaurs* (1999) moved us a little further along. But at the end of this particular pathway is the 'imaginary' and not the observed 'real'. The sophistication, effectiveness, or plausibility of the dinosaurs on screen is judged within its comparison with the sub-sub-genre of the computer-animated dinosaur film, whether it claims to be documentary or entertaining in effect. For all any of us know (and I stress the 'know') all dinosaurs hopped and bounced about the landscape like squealing schoolchildren at playtime. Or had perpetual hiccups. Or had polka dot markings. I 'know' how they should move and look on screen, but I do not 'know' how they did move and should look in life. We might 'suppose' or even 'deduce' things from the fossil record, but we do not 'know' if and how simulation matches real. No human observed the creatures in question, and the prehistoric is best known for its lack of record keeping even when there was a human presence. It is a disappointment encountered by every schoolboy that no recognisable ancestor feasted on brontosaur steaks or ran from a marauding Tyrannosaurus rex. Use of flocking algorithms based on the observation of the flight of birds to model the behaviour of dinosaurs can only simulate the flocking of birds – otherwise we are left with the possible and the 'imaginary', whatever the stridency of the claims for the 'real' made by those who will take observation of one event to another. This takes nothing away from the images with which we are confronted, however. They are aesthetically pleasing, they offer the pleasure of spectacle, and there is something simply 'fun' about walking around the grazing dinosaurs or staring up at the wheeling pterodactyls in *Gunman Chronicles* before everything goes haywire and the running and shooting begins in earnest.

This is not to deny that the technology, rather than the deployment of technology within the computer game, cannot be read as posing a 'threat' to a distinction that is already under strain. The same technology that is used by the computer game obviously has the potential to deceive, and probably not too far in the future, if it has not done so already. But there again, so has the technology of the printed word, the technology of film, and the technology of television. I do not deny this potential, but would ask that we not leap too quickly to an assumption that the possibility for deceit demands more than the critical reading of such texts. We should learn to recognise what is self-evident 'fact' and what is self-evident 'fiction'. If we do not, we invite deception. But this is more an argument for considered and informed reading, and not blanket condemnation or even 'fear' of the computer game. We do not reject or condemn the fictional products communicated through the printed word because of the possibility of the criminal forgery, ignore the filmic text because its potential for deceit has been abused by some terrifying regimes, or stop ourselves from watching junk TV because it has consistently confirmed the *X-Files* maxim that 'the truth is out there' rather than within its own programming.

The basic point I make again and again by implication in this volume is that it is not always necessary, or even advisable, to turn immediately to the work of critics such as Baudrillard, Jameson, Hassan, or Umberto Eco (whose own discussion of 'hyperreality' similarly offers tempting connections) when confronted with the formal novelty of the computer game.[14] In a sense, we should not get too excited (yet), we should not rush to declare that we occupy a new age of representation (yet). There is something new here, and something new in its emergence from the technological moment at which we are now placed, but it is not a new phenomenon that is ahistorical in its form or its reference. The game-fiction has not sprung fully formed from the depths of the machine, and the search for a radical break from previous modes of representation is likely to be futile, as is any assumption that it is only the cutting edge of contemporary critical theory that can inform our consideration of such a contemporary form. Rather, the need is (perhaps paradoxically) for us to locate the computer game in relation to other forms of fiction – to suppress this temptation to make correspondences of language stand in for actual correspondence, and to look in the first instance not for the philosophical questions the computer game might raise at some time in the future, but closely at the things themselves.

What is surprising, perhaps, is the degree to which it is possible to approach such texts in a critically sophisticated fashion without merely being left with a category statement. If we engage in the careful business of close textual analysis rather than leap immediately into the realms of speculative theory we might not just apply a convenient label, but recognise its formal novelty. In offering up the admittedly ugly coinage 'game-fiction' to describe the texts under scrutiny, I hope to communicate the narrowness of my enquiry and not just make my own error of reductive taxonomy. This is a work concerned with those computer games that I see as having a central narrative impetus, that develop story over time, rather than simply repeat with minimal difference in a move from level to level of increasing excess. Such a neologism signals a rejection of the alternatives as much as anything particularly startling about my specific examples. 'Videogame' overstresses sight with no reference to cognitive understanding, and the term I have used up until this point, 'computer game', speaks of the technology rather than the text. I am also aware that it is the personal computer, rather than the arcade cabinet, the games console linked to a television set, or the hand-held console with its minimal memory and tiny screen that I am interested in here. In part this is because I am interested in the multiplicity of utility (that consoles are moving to emulate) of the personal computer that sits on desks at home and at work, and particularly the ways in which this workhorse of labour in the early twenty-first century is where we read computer-based texts both for work and for fun. It is possible that one form of literacy (how we read the computer-based texts of the Internet, for example), might come to cross-pollinate with this other form of literacy in which I am interested – how we read game-fictions.

Reading game-fictions

The concentration in this study on notions of authenticity and realism, beyond keeping it to a manageable size, should allow me to address another prevalent temptation. The sometimes understandable confusion that appears to exist in the popular mind, and particularly the popular press, regarding the effect of such simulations in the real world, and the supposed blurring of distinctions between game-worlds and the real world generate all sorts of negative comment. Too many things become confused, too many correspondences are made and generalisations allowed to stand without sufficient scrutiny. The remotely piloted vehicle used for space or deep-sea exploration, or for entry into hazardous environments such as the inside of nuclear reactors, is now a reality. It will not be long before such machines are deployed by the US military for first-strike missions. For all I know, they exist already. The interface between controller and real environment in such circumstances is often similar to that between player and game environment. As the use of video footage as part of the public relations offensive during Operation Desert Storm indicated, these all too real computerised interventions in the real world share many of the characteristics of their gaming cousins. Anecdotal and press accounts of more general confusion can range from the worrying (such as a USAAF mechanic who is rumoured to have learnt to fly a state of the art warplane using a flight simulator on his PC and then taken a real plane for a joyride), to the alarming (and possibly alarmist) tales of teenagers preparing for mass shootings using custom-designed levels for first-person shooting games that replicate the geography of their school buildings.

The relationship between fictional representation and real world acts of violence, whether supposedly inspired by films, novels, or computer games, is a notoriously thorny issue, but this formal examination of the computer game *as* fictional form is intended to clarify some of the general issues that are rarely addressed. Too many simplistic associations are allowed to pass without sufficient examination (players of *Tekken 3* (1998) or *Street Fighter* (2000) are more violent in the real world than those who play *Ecco the Dolphin* (2000), perhaps), and the fictional status of the game and the necessity of the player's recognition of that fictionality, is obscured. And there also seems to be some inconsistency in the responses generated by this form of fiction compared to the responses that greet other forms. The 'realistic' violence of the opening Normandy landing sequence of the film *Saving Private Ryan* (1998) was critically praised: the 'realism' of first-person shooting games is often subject to condemnation and potential censorship.

It should always be remembered that however much the computer game might be (and particularly have the potential to be) 'more than a game', it is still a fictional form. As a form of mass entertainment, like punk, rock and roll, and the novel before it, the computer game has been seen as offering some sort of threat to society, particularly by providing a space in which otherwise taboo or outlawed behaviour (spitting and swearing, the sexual expression of pelvic gyration, adultery, and aggression as the first resort in problem solving) is given free range. But the confusion of game for real is indicative of individual dysfunction and 'misreading' just as much as the confusion of the films *A Clockwork Orange* (1971) or *Natural-Born Killers* (1994) with a template for real behaviour is a misreading. This is fiction, and should be treated, and subject to rigorous examination, just as other forms of fiction are. Its fictionality does not remove the need for the development of an understanding of how it works.

In undertaking a primarily formal analysis of computer games within this book I have restricted myself to the discussion of a fairly narrow range of games that constitute variants of what I term game-fictions. The most interesting contemporary game-fictions, at least for the purposes of this study, are those that borrow heavily from literary and cinematic conventions in the construction of something that resembles a game/fiction hybrid

(*Tomb Raider*, *Half-Life*), games that offer a fictional intersection with historical event in the creation of a species of historical fiction (*Close Combat*), and games that allow for the creation and management of fictional social constructions (*SimCity*). Without being overly reductive, and while I fully recognise the fluidity of genre distinctions in such a young and rapidly developing field, my interest is in those genres of games that appear to have the potential to develop into something approximating the sophistication of the currently culturally dominant forms of popular fiction: novels, films, and television programmes. I might be treating those 'shoot-'em-ups' that develop story seriously, but I will be avoiding talking at any length about those 'beat-'em-ups' that seem to go nowhere else other than towards 'let's-beat-'em-up-some-more'.

Somewhere in the storytelling of the game-fictions I focus upon, I see fictional possibility and fictional promise.[15] As the advance of communication and print technology was intimately related to the rise of the novel, and technological advance was inseparable from the development of cinema and television, so one cannot ignore the potential for advances in this new fictional form that may yet accompany this truly startling rise in computer processing power. Given that rise, to assume that the computer game will always be the junior partner in the relationship between itself and other fictional forms might well be naive.[16] The example offered by those would-be futurologists of the middle of the last century who predicted atomic powered cars, colonies on Mars, and a diet consisting entirely of brightly coloured pills by the year 2000 is salutary, and I do not want to offer too many such hostages to fortune in this volume. But it is already possible to foresee a not too distant future in which the progress of processor technology, if combined with the creative flair we are used to seeing applied in our other forms of popular entertainment, could lead to the development of a generation of games that transcend the pejorative classification of children's entertainment and are taken as seriously as mass-appeal novels and films occasionally are. It would not take too much of a leap of the imagination to see the computer game develop into something like a new form of soap opera or action movie. One day, perhaps, the computer game will even produce its *À la Recherche du Temps Perdu* or its *Ulysses*, its *Casablanca* or its *Citizen Kane*. It is, as yet, early days, and this is a reading of those early days.

Notes

1 Ernest Hemingway, *A Farewell To Arms* (London: Grafton, 1977 [1929]), p. 133.

2 Jon Covey (ed.), *Fractal Dreams: New Media in Social Context* (London: Lawrence and Wishart, 1996), p. xii. See also Kevin Robins 'Cyberspace and the World We Live In' in the same volume, pp. 1–30.

3 A useful introduction to narratological theory can be found in Steven Cohan and Linda M. Shires, *Telling Stories: A Theoretical Analysis of Narrative Fiction* (London: Routledge, 1988). For an account that then takes narratological analysis to film, and which is therefore of much relevance in the examination of such a visually dependent medium as the computer game, see Jakob Lothe, *Narrative in Fiction and Film: An Introduction* (New York and Oxford: Oxford University Press, 2000).

4 Jean Baudrillard, 'Aesthetic Illusion and Virtual Reality' in *Reading Images*, ed. Julia Thomas (Basingstoke: Palgrave, 2001), pp. 198–206.

5 Walter Benjamin, 'The Work of Art in the Age of Mechanical Reproduction' trans. Harry Zohn, in *Illuminations: Essays and Reflections* (London: Cape, 1970), pp. 211–44. I will return to a consideration of Benjamin's essay in Chapter 6.

6 Baudrillard, 'The Ecstasy of Communication' in Hal Foster (ed.), *Postmodern Culture* (London: Pluto, 1985), pp. 126–34, p. 127.

7 Fredric Jameson, 'Postmodernism and Consumer Society' in Foster (ed.), *Postmodern Culture*, pp. 111–25. As Jameson notes in an all too often ignored, and still relevant, opening statement, 'The concept of postmodernism is not widely accepted or even understood today' (p. 111). That the postmodern is the site of debate rather than certainty and has been misrepresented as a straightforward category statement in popular usage has also been reiterated recently in Simon Malpas's introduction to his *Postmodern Debates* (Basingstoke: Palgrave, 2001),

a valuable book that includes many of the key essays that have contributed to our understanding of what the multiple meanings of the postmodern might be.

8 Ihab Hassan, 'Towards a Concept of Postmodernism' in Thomas Docherty (ed.), *Postmodernism: A Reader* (New York and London: Harvester, 1995), pp. 146–56, p. 152. See also Hassan's *The Dismemberment of Orpheus: Towards a Postmodern Literature* (New York and Oxford: Oxford University Press, 1982).

9 And yet I would not want to make any easy moves to accommodate theoretical models that have a superficial correspondence because they have discussed other 'games' in other contexts. For those conversant with psychoanalytic theory, for example, Sigmund Freud's discussion of the 'fort/da' game provides a case in point. See James Strachey (ed.), *Beyond the Pleasure Principle* (New York: Norton, 1961). I can imagine an attractive and potentially elegant argument that really does little more than ignore Freud's grounding of his conclusions about the child's game of the disposal and recovery of a toy in observation, and simply substitutes the loss/recovery of the cherished object with the loss ('death')/recovery (reload) of the protagonist of the game-fiction. One can then simply move from the discussion of what is specific to gameplay within game-fictions to making more general assertions about the form. This is not the case in this study.

10 The terms are Roland Barthes from *S/Z*, trans. Richard Miller (New York: Hill and Wang, 1975). Barthes is, like Benjamin, another 'absent presence' beneath much of the argument in this work: as a champion of semiology; as an exceptionally astute reader of popular culture texts (see *Mythologies* trans. Annette Lavers (London: Paladin, 1972); and as author of *The Pleasure of the Text*, trans. Richard Miller (Oxford: Blackwell, 1990). I do not have space to tease out the significance of his arguments in the last of these works in full here, but would recommend that any reader interested in pursuing the prioritisation of the pleasure of reading in game-fiction consult this volume.

11 Gérard Genette, *Narrative Discourse: An Essay in Method*, trans. Jane E. Lewin (Ithaca, NY: Cornell University Press, 1980). See also *Palimpsests: Literature in the Second Degree*, trans. Channa Newman and Claude Doubinsky (Lincoln, NE: University of Nebraska Press, 1997).

A coherent and informed account of Genette's thinking in this area can be found in Graham Allen, *Intertextuality* (London: Routledge, 2000) pp. 95–132.

12 Baudrillard, 'The Precession of Simulacra', in Brian Wallis (ed.) *Art After Modernism: Rethinking Representation* (New York: New York Museum of Contemporary Art, 1984), pp. 253–82, p. 254.

13 The phrase 'consensual hallucination' is William Gibson's from *Neuromancer* (London: Gollancz, 1984), p. 12. The extent to which such consensus relies on consent, and therefore on a willed knowing that one agrees to the terms of that consent relates most closely to the discussion of 'immersion' in Chapter 3 of this work.

14 For a collection of essays that looks at Eco's understanding of the 'hyperreal' (that differs from Baudrillard's) in the context of popular culture, see Umberto Eco, *Travels in Hyperreality* trans. William Weaver and Christine Leefeldt (London: Picador, 1987).

15 Another obvious absence from consideration I will admit to, however, is the multiplayer game. This is not simply a response to the technological limitations imposed by slow Internet connections at the time of writing, that have meant that the number of players within the UK remains relatively insignificant. There are interesting things going on as more and more computer games come bundled with a multi-player option, and new generations of consoles move to provide Internet connections, but this book, with its emphasis on how the reading experience offered by game-fiction texts can be related to the reading experience offered by other forms of narrative fiction, is not the place for their interrogation.

16 For those who like statistics, Steven Poole makes his case with the support of some startlingly large numbers in the opening sections of *Trigger Happy: The Inner Life of Videogames* (London: Fourth Estate, 2000). Just to add one more number to Poole's, there is something extraordinary in the claim made by *Tomb Raider*'s producers as they moved towards release of another episode in 2002 of twenty-eight million units sold by that date. One only has to multiply that number by the average retail price of the computer game to realise just how significant the computer game has become in terms of an economic (if not necessarily cultural) phenomenon.

2

Fantastically real: reading *Tomb Raider*

Tomb Raider [inc. *Tomb Raider* (1996), *Tomb Raider II: The Dagger of Xian* (1997), *Tomb Raider III: The Adventures of Lara Croft* (1998), *Tomb Raider: The Last Revelation* (1999), *Tomb Raider: Chronicles* (2000)] Third-person action/adventure. The player controls the actions (running, jumping, walking, climbing, crawling, shooting etc.) of Lara Croft, usually from a third-person perspective. Progress through the game involves frequent jumping of the protagonist from platform to platform. Jump distances are often precise, and measured according to a system of blocks of standard size that make up the in-game landscape. That landscape is realised so as to allow the illusion of three dimensions in which the protagonist can be moved. The games involve a series of quests for various objects that must be retrieved after overcoming obstacles. These might be broadly categorised as either puzzles or adversaries. The emphasis, however, is largely on the use of a range of weapons.

The title of this chapter is offered as more than a weak pun, and with a full awareness that it begins with what appears to be a contradiction in terms. *Tomb Raider* is not, and does not make any claim to be, concerned with the real. Like well-written prose, we may admire its technical achievement, but we do not risk being so taken in by this fiction that we mistake it for fact. Nor does the increasing visual sophistication of the games within the series necessarily amount to an eliding of difference between text and real: the inclusion of ever more fine detail within the game landscape does not imply that we are coming ever closer to the replication of the real. We may become deeply involved in the experience of watching or playing 'as' Lara Croft, but we never undertake a magical transformation to 'become' her.[1] This is a fantasy world forever mediated not just by a distance between player and protagonist that is integral to the third-person gameplay (we 'look' not so much over her shoulder, but from above and behind), but by the technology of delivery. When the rain slants down in the opening sequence of *Tomb Raider III* we are in no danger of seeing Lara Croft give an involuntary electronic shudder, or of seeing her pony-tail become sodden and heavy when she emerges from one of her many swimming expeditions. She drips briefly, but this is a visual gesture that has no further effect. There is no such thing as a bad hair day in *Tomb Raider*. Such refinements may be coming in a future episode, and are considered in more detail in the discussion of *Half-Life* in Chapter 3, but whatever the technology harnessed, whatever the ingenuity of the programmers, and whatever the computing power deployed, this will remain an essentially stylised representational version of something that is other than real experience.

What limited claims the game's promoters do make for realism are essentially comparative with other computer games. This game is *more* realistic than earlier platform jumping games such as *Super Mario* or *Donkey Kong*. To draw on the language in which realism is commonly discussed, then its most basic claim to be more realistic than such earlier computer games is that it is not as 'flat' or 'two dimensional', and offers the illusion of three dimensions (at least in terms of the rendering of landscape, if not of character and plot). The *Tomb Raider* landscape 'grid' is always visible, and its visibility is essential to the working out of possible moves. If we make comparisons with other forms of fiction, rather than with other computer games, then *Tomb Raider* is undeniably primitive, and the reader of this form of fiction understands the limitations of its realism just as he or she recognises the supporting architectural grid of the in-game landscape. There is a certain type of movie-goer who takes extreme pleasure in locating breakdowns in the cinematic illusion of the real (the digital watch on the wrist of the extra in the crowd scene of a swords and sandals Roman epic, the wobbling polystyrene gravestone set moving by a passing Penguin in *Batman Returns* (1992)), but no one gets similarly excited by the glaring continuity error of an immaculately coiffured Lara Croft emerging bone dry from the water.[2]

Tomb Raider's self-evident artificiality is not in itself a failing that would necessitate its exclusion from the genre of realist game-fictions identified in this study. No critic of the novel or of film would be particularly exercised by the distance that always remains between representation and real, and the essential 'illusionism' of what is commonly termed realism.[3] If the trick of illusion is performed with skill and panache, then we are entitled to applaud, whether we are confronted with a passage of elegant prose, a well-directed scene, or even an impressive moment of gameplay. The nod and a wink to fictionality that features so often in contemporary films and novels that accept and make obvious their own fictionality, and is also a feature of *Tomb Raider*, is intended to spark a certain frisson of complicity in the reader or viewer. That the trick's methodology might be visible can add to, rather than detract from, the experience of reading. It certainly does not render an otherwise realist text somehow unreadable. What is meant by realism here, then, places the emphasis on the 'ism' as much as on the 'real', and is intended to suggest that the 'world' offered by the game is itself internally consistent, realistic in its own terms and according to its conventions. To make this claim is no more radical than claiming that it is possible to locate a core realist impulse within those novels that make such play with the acknowledgement of their status as novels. For those with the inclination, examples can be found in almost any works by Salman Rushdie, Gabriel Garcia Marquez, or Angela Carter, among others.[4] After all, the putative critic of game-fiction must surely be as entitled to the sub-genre of fantastic realism as the literary critic is to his or her magical realism.

The questions of form examined in this chapter follow from the central premise that *Tomb Raider* can be 'read' as fiction, and as self-conscious fiction in which serious play is made not just in game terms, but in terms that literary critics would recognise as play with the possibilities and limitations of storytelling. Some aspects of this self-consciousness, it is demonstrated here, are the result of what might be termed deliberate 'authorial' intention or design, and include (but sometimes go beyond) mere parody and pastiche. Potentially more interesting formal characteristics emerge, with the game designers' conscious help or without it, from the meeting of technology with what I variously refer to as 'reader' as well as 'player'. In taking in such questions as how this fiction 'works' in a formal sense, and what the relationship is between this fictional mode and the other fictional modes it draws upon and alludes to, I hope to justify my claim that the *Tomb Raider* series is a representative, however primitive, of a new fictional form.

Lara Croft: action hero

One consequence of the unusual cross-media penetration enjoyed by *Tomb Raider* has been the transition of Lara Croft from the object of a substantial advertising and marketing campaign, to the vehicle for the promotion of another product. There is even some potential irony in the choice of product that 'her' digital image is used to promote, an energy drink that markets itself on its ability to revitalise a flagging human constitution. The Lucozade campaign, which appeared in the United Kingdom throughout 2000, blatantly acknowledges something that is implied again and again in the games themselves: Lara Croft's fictionality. And in its television manifestation at least, it does so by offering another layer of knowing fiction. In the advertisement a player halts a game to attend, presumably, to some human need or other. The action stops, as it must do, when he leaves his console. But the game-world is not frozen as a consequence of the lack of human input. Lara Croft and her digital adversaries are not frozen on screen, but take a well-deserved break. She drinks the product she is endorsing and, refreshed, is ready to continue with the drama upon the return of the player. Several observations spring immediately to mind. Lara Croft is presented, here, no matter how archly, as having a form of existence independent of the player. In this context she is not associated with that other fictional world of the series of games which operate within and through their own internal logic (and in which she is an 'archaeologist-adventurer'), but with another fictional alternative entirely, and one carrying another set of expectations, that of film.

Even though the live-action film version of *Tomb Raider* had yet to go into production, 'Lara Croft' was already acknowledged as a role to be played. The advertisers did not choose to have Lara Croft played by a human actor: this digital Lara Croft is a digital actor. Not only does this conceit that Lara Croft is some kind of 'cyber-babe' starlet, as she has sometimes been characterised in the popular press (even appearing in 'glamour' shots alongside ostensibly real models in *Loaded* magazine) presumably help to shift units, but it also emphasises the manner in which she has come to escape some of the more narrow confines of the computer game as the preserve of adolescents and the socially dysfunctional. Somehow she has entered into a wider public consciousness as icon and image as familiar to a certain age group as any number of Hollywood starlets. She might still be most recognisable to small boys and young men, but she was certainly one of the first widely recognisable 'characters' of computer fictions. The game's publishers had recognised this aspect of their creation as early as on the blurb on the box of *Tomb Raider II*, on which the phrase 'starring Lara Croft' appears five times immediately beneath the main title.

Some of the implications of this intensity of cinematic allusion for *Tomb Raider*'s realism and its relationship with other fictional forms are clear. Ms Croft's antics are no more 'real' than those of any other feature film action hero. She, and the chainsaw-wielding muscle man who is initially chasing her before the action is halted, are only acting. Their mutual antipathy is a fiction. The vicious Dobermans that had also joined the chase are only playing a role. This advertisement plays with the conventions of the knowing self-consciousness of so much contemporary film, television and (particularly) advertising where the seriousness of any genre's claims to be replicating a plausibly realistic other world are deliberately undercut and rendered problematic.

The player within the world of the advertisement might be 'fooled' into thinking that he has control over the actions of the game's hero, but we, the viewers, are given a privileged sight of the 'true' nature of the hero as actor playing a role within a particular kind of fiction, the action movie. He is, in a limited sense, 'directing' the action in a fashion of which he does not appear aware. Which is where, of course, things get a little complicated. Alongside all this playful manipulation with the expectations of various fictional forms, there is little chance of anyone mistaking this Lara Croft for a 'real' human being. *Tomb Raider* stars Lara Croft playing the role of … Lara Croft. Her features are stylised, even within the enforced angularity of the available technology, and her body shape (as has so often been noted) is implausibly engineered to cater for the assumed fantasies, if not expectations, of a largely male adolescent audience. There are obvious reasons why the advertisers choose to make the player of the game 'he' rather than 'she'. The euphemistic phrase 'featuring an enhanced Lara Croft', again from the box notes of *Tomb Raider II*, refers to a form of 'enhancement' that would be familiar to any Californian cosmetic surgeon. But it is not her fictive nature as a visual construct with an exaggerated body image produced through the mapping of digital information that is foregrounded here, but her fictive nature as another example of the action hero that we recognise from film. An audience familiar with Lara Croft's computer game incarnation might be amused, entertained, or indifferent to the shift across media and the blurring of boundaries between her performance within game/televisual/cinematic conventions, but they would hardly be shocked. There has always been something of a cinematic quality to *Tomb Raider*.

The most obvious debt that the *Tomb Raider* games themselves owe to film is indicated in the title of the series, and if that is not enough to remind any player of the Indiana Jones movies starring Harrison Ford, then the presence of the occasional rolling ball, spiked traps, comic-book villainous exotic others, and items of mystical significance (the Dagger of Xian and the Armour of Set in place of the Ark of the Covenant and the Holy Grail, among others) should ring the correct intertextual bells. Even the core premise of Lara Croft's adventures, as she engages in a rather muscular form of 'archaeology' that is some distance from what is understood to be common practice in university archaeology departments, is recognisable as one more borrowing from Spielberg's creation. If further proof were needed of the debt owed by the *Tomb Raider* designers to the example of Indiana Jones, then it might be found in the reversal of influence evident in the *Tomb Raider*-like jumping and lever-pulling gameplay that featured in the belated release of *Indiana Jones and the Infernal Machine* (1999).

Tomb Raider, and Lara Croft, is also more than just a rather aggressive Indiana Jones without the whip, and the series finds its inspiration (or, if we were to be theoretically generous, its intertexts) in many places. In its reference to films ranging from horror to gangster to science fiction to kung fu to dinosaur films, among many others, *Tomb Raider* is cheerfully eclectic. *Tomb Raider* is as ready to plunder the visual vocabulary of a wide range of film genres as Lara Croft is ready to plunder whatever building or cave or temple she finds herself in. Mummies shamble forward, muscular thugs tote Uzi sub-machine guns, ninjas spin and twirl, dinosaurs either thud forward menacingly (the T-rex in *Tomb Raider II*) or move with lithe agility (the 'Raptors' in *Tomb Raider III*) in a fashion suspiciously familiar from the live action/computer animation hybrid *Jurassic Park*.

If one were simply to play the often vacuous game of identifying intertexts, then even the most basic consideration of the game's gun-wielding, athletic, and attractive hero should bring to mind the 'strong women' of Sigourney Weaver's Ripley from the *Alien* series (1979, 1986, 1992, 1997) and even the eponymous heroes of Ridley Scott's *Thelma and Louise* (1991). And it is worth noting in passing that some of *Tomb Raider*'s general appeal might have its source in its allusion to such figures: a move that allows a veneer of (post)feminist respectability in the portrayal of a 'strong' and independent female lead character in what remains, in essence, a 'shoot-'em-up'.

But *Tomb Raider*'s designers are not just borrowers of plots and props, the fine detail, or even the basic premise of such films. Instead, they deploy some of the techniques of film-making themselves. And, as film is something other than the visual replication of lived experience as if what happens on screen were simply an alternative 'real' visual experience, so this game requires its audience, reader, or player, to acknowledge a complex formal grammar in order to be able to read it. Much of the time spent playing *Tomb Raider* leaves the player fixed at a point directly behind its protagonist, directing actions from non-omniscient distance. The usual cinematic variation of shifts from close-up to long-shot has some echo within the game, and a few keystrokes shift the point of view to that of the protagonist herself. In the later games binoculars and night-sights allow close-ups of the game landscape rendered through the formal cinematic and televisual convention of the circle of focus surrounded by black space. Such points of view, essential to the gameplay methodology of the series, are joined, however, by far more interesting moments in which cinematic and game modes merge.

The most obvious importation of cinematic strategies can be found in the cut-scenes, those excerpts of computer animation (often referred to as FMV, or Full-Motion Video sequences) that replicate cinema film in an obvious way. Such formal set-pieces serve to move what little plot there is along, acting most often as buffer-zones between essentially similar spaces in which the player will still have little freedom of movement beyond the usual walk, run, sprint, swim, jump, grab, push alternatives. They provide what basic characterisation there is in such games, as well as allowing the protagonist the opportunity of indulging in the same kind of lame and scripted wise-cracks that pass for humour in the action movies of Arnold Schwarzenneger, Bruce Willis etc. In some ways they are similar to those often tiresome pauses between frenetic action in which plot is explained slowly and carefully to both protagonist and audience in a certain kind of action movie. In addition there is often evidence of a display of the programmer's technical virtuosity, an attempt to push the limits of what is realisable within the technology of the moment that generates the same aesthetic appreciation as the finely realised illusion of the skilled draughtsman or painter, or, to draw a closer analogy, the purely technical level of achievement that has contributed to the success of computer-animated films such as Disney's *Toy Story* (1995) or *Toy Story 2* (1999), or Pixar's *Antz* (1998) and still informs discussion of each successive wave of movies of increasing technical sophistication.

One partial example of such an FMV cut-scene should suffice to demonstrate their essentially cinematic quality, as well as their often derivative character. *Tomb Raider: The Last Revelation* opens with a level designed to introduce the player to the major possible moves that the protagonist can make. An adolescent Lara Croft jumps and runs and climbs according to the instructions of a substitute father figure, the self-styled archaeologist-adventurer Werner Von Croy. For once, and presumably because of her tender age, she is denied the arsenal of weapons she usually has access to. Upon completion of the level, in which Lara Croft and Werner Von Croy have raced to recover an item known as the 'Iris' from a temple complex in Angkor Wat, control of Lara's actions is removed from the player and an FMV sequence rolls. In a manner reminiscent of the squabbling between the two Doctors Jones in the second Indiana Jones film, Lara Croft shows caution about pulling the lever that will expose the Iris from its concealment within a globe-like structure, while Werner Von Croy is impatient and calls on his greater experience and maturity to persuade her to do as he commands. This is how what follows is described on one of the many unofficial *Tomb Raider* sites that exist on the Internet:

> Lara pulls the lever, and the globe opens like a sliced orange revealing the Iris as a walkway descends to create a path from the outer ledge to the center of the now open globe. Von Croy walks out to the center of the now opened globe and reaches to pick up the Iris.

> Von Croy: 'Have faith in experience child and you will learn more than simple …'

> Von Croy stops talking as the entire structure trembles. Lara struggles to stay on her feet and says: 'As you were saying?'[5]

An earthquake tips Werner Von Croy over, and his leg is caught on one of the segments of the globe. He is left dangling in space as the globe segments begin to close. Lara Croft at first attempts to run away, then has a moment of conscience and makes a futile effort to help, and finally barely escapes as the temple is sealed with Werner Von Croy still trapped inside the globe. One last plaintive cry of 'Werner' and the action fades. Cut to a long sequence in which a 'mysterious' female figure investigates ruins in the desert until the legend 'Egypt, present day' appears on screen.

What we have here, then, is immediately recognisable as a method of plot establishment and advancement that makes the most of some of the graphics capabilities of the game engine in the replication of a cinematic experience. The camera had been active throughout the cut scene, mood music had set the forbidding scene, and the geometric form of the globe had enabled some fairly impressive, and yet not too complex, animation. In story terms, Lara's maturity is marked by her recognition of the fallibility of her mentor/father figure and her spotless moral credentials are established as she looks back on the apparent entombment of Von Croy with as much regret as the programmers' limited visual palette and the girlish voice-over can generate. A rivalry and grudge is established between Werner Von Croy and Lara Croft (for we *know* he is not dead, just as we *know* Lara will escape at the last moment) that will drive a particular kind of plot forward. As a bonus, the cut-scene also provides a logical explanation for the walking stick and limp that join Von Croy's middle-European accent and his wire-frame glasses as sure signs of his villainous status.

Whether this is simply 'bad' fiction, or undertaken with tongue firmly in cheek in the spirit of parody or pastiche, is largely irrelevant. Indeed, what it foregrounds most forcefully is the weakness of FMV as the delivery system of an interactive or collaborative (human *and* computer) form of fiction. Instead it suggests that what one gets in contemporary computer games is a level of dialogue that is laughably predictable, and a mobilisation of clichés that might make even some of Hollywood's finest action movie directors squirm.

Of all the more cinematic digressions from gameplay, however, the cut-scenes are probably the least interesting in formal terms as game-fiction gives way to a form of ersatz movie-making in which the player has minimal investment or involvement. One area where cinema and gameplay merge without the abrupt, complete and extended loss of player control, and the associated elimination of the illusion of freedom of action, is in the movement of the in-game camera and angle of shot, and the use of the sound track to heighten tension. At its simplest, this sees the vision of the protagonist and/or the player directed towards some otherwise missable space or object, or a shift in background music or noises alerts the player to the imminent arrival of an adversary. At its most complex, entry into a new area sees the in-game camera move away from the protagonist and engage in the kind of long travelling shot usually to be found in big-budget Hollywood productions. Even in miniature, such as during the 'death-slide' sequence of *Tomb Raider II*, when the full depth of the canyon below is revealed in a sweeping camera shot, this can be impressive. Through such sequences the player might, again, enjoy a privileged view of otherwise obscured levers, blocks, doorways, or traps, and plot points might be made, but the effect is often primarily one of the generation of aesthetic enjoyment, and the dropping of hints about how to proceed is combined with an often spectacular technical realisation of the game world. The sight of a low-flying Stealth Bomber passing at close quarters in the Area 51 section of *Tomb Raider III*, for example, does not merely signal the kind of adversaries the player is about to face, but is undeniably impressive in and of itself.

At its most successfully realised, such as in the Venice section of *Tomb Raider II*, such a merging of cinematic visual realisation with gameplay interaction by the player results in the production of something akin to a personal mini-movie, a cinematic vignette that is only produced as a result of, or reward for, player interaction. Such moments conceal the shift from active to passive participant 'in' the action. Having explored the limits of Venice and opened doors and cleared obstacles in the standard fashion of such games, the player is left in a position where he or she must race a speedboat through the canals in a race against the clock before the exit to the next area is closed. The debt that the level designers and programmers owe to the cinematic exploits of James Bond become obvious as the speedboat clears two ramps to land on a line of gondolas, swings through a narrow passage and hurtles through the level's exit gate to the accompaniment of the last few chimes of the bell that had signalled the countdown. Although there are alternative methods of movement from the Venice canals area into the next area (and I shall return to consideration of their implications a little later in this chapter), none are as aesthetically pleasing or so fully demonstrate one possibly unique kind of fiction that can be created within such game-fictions. It is the initial concealment of this series of discrete moves, the piecing together of clues as obscure as any found in detective fiction, with all the readerly pleasure that accompanies such delayed disclosure within text, that leads to the final reward of the fully realised sequence. Unlike the cut-scene FMV sequences there is no single trigger that transforms player into viewer, and this moment of gaming cinema requires the continuing active participation of the player if it is to be successfully realised.

Tomb Raider as quest narrative

For all the claims made here that one can see the first stirrings of a new fictional form within *Tomb Raider*, it should not be forgotten that it owes just as much, if not more, to other forms of game as it does to other forms of fiction such as film. One basic genealogy that also highlights the 'fantasy' rather than 'realist' roots of the game might trace a line of descent from those fantasy wargames played with cast-metal miniatures of orcs and dwarves and dragons, through table-top role-playing games, making the leap into its first digital incarnation in the text-based adventures that appeared on such early dedicated games machines as the ZX Spectrum (and who will ever truly forget the frustration of playing the pioneering Spectrum adventure *The Hobbit* (1982), and being told, yet again, that 'Thorin sits down and starts singing about gold'?) Text-based adventures suffered in comparison with more visually sophisticated games, and the virtually static 'point and click' adventures that emerged out of adventures like *The Hobbit* seem to have been all but superseded by *Tomb Raider* and its imitators.

Any such formal system of rules that govern interaction between players inevitably have much in common with the 'rules' of storytelling. Table-top role-playing, perhaps still most commonly associated with the sub-Tolkienesque 'Dungeons and Dragons' (a game-system that has since made a commercially successful transition to computer format, notably in its incarnation as *Baldur's Gate* (1998)) has, particularly, had its fair share of claims made for it that it represents a 'new' form of storytelling. In such a game the players interact through speech (rather than necessarily by moving pieces on any kind of board) with a game environment controlled by a referee-cum-mediator usually termed a 'Dungeon Master'. The interaction between players and referee could, theoretically, lead to the creation of a free-form story in which, allowing only for the internal logic of the game and its rules, almost anything might happen. The illusion of near-total freedom of action that such games allowed in the abstract was, however, often at odds with the restrictive reality of many of the commercially available supplements and adventures. In many ways these bore more than a passing resemblance to the levels to be found in *Tomb Raider*: underground rooms and passages (the 'Dungeon') populated by traps, adversaries and the occasional helper who must variously be disarmed, overcome, or persuaded to offer aid. All too often, these games descended (at least in personal memory) into little more than a sequence of 'open the door, kill the monster, grab the gold, open the next door, kill the monster, grab the gold …' The more formulaic of such games also gave rise to what one would have to hesitate to term 'literary' by-products in game-books that rarely transcended something like the following (imaginary) example:

> *You have entered a room in the dungeon in which there is an extremely ugly creature asleep on a bed of straw. Beside it is a sword, and it is curled up around a pile of gold.* Do you:
>
> Attack the creature? (Go to page 24)
>
> Attempt to steal the gold without waking the monster? (Go to page 116)
>
> Return the way you came as quietly as you can? (Curse yourself for your cowardice and then go to page 11)

Tolstoy, or even Tolkien, it wasn't.

Tomb Raider shares this propensity towards a linear passage forwards with an extended but similarly finite range of options for moving the action along. Part of the immaturity of computer games as fictional form alluded to in Chapter 1 can be located in the extent to which animate problems (or 'other people') are best 'resolved' in that fashion memorably described by Harrison Ford's pre-Indiana Jones character in *Apocalypse Now* (1979) as termination 'with extreme prejudice'. Pacifism, or even kindness to animals, has little place within this fictional world. In *Tomb Raider*, if it moves your best option is usually to kill it, and the expectation according to the internal logic of the game is that you should do so. If something does not move, and yet appears to differ from the decorative eye-candy of the surrounding walls and ceiling (levers, pulleys, ropes, differently shaded blocks, differently textured surfaces), then it can usually be moved, manipulated, or climbed. The separation of significant detail from insignificant detail is not just a contributor to readerly pleasure in game-fictions (as it is, for example, in the recognition of the detective novel's 'red herrings') but is essential to the furthering of plot (as if the reading of detective fiction would grind to a halt until the correct discrimination is made between clue and red herring). At its crudest, this kind of gameplay can be just as formulaic as that found in the fantasy game-books, and, when one has exhausted all the pushing and pulling possibilities available, the player is usually left with no alternatives but walking onwards or making a number of jumps of standardised length and height to gain access to new areas of the level.

Radical alternatives are rarely allowed in normal gameplay, although there are several moments when going in with all guns blazing is less than advisable (leaving monkeys alive in *Tomb Raider III* can allow them to lead the player to less than obvious locations; not shooting any of the monks in the Tibetan monastery in *Tomb Raider II* makes the game a lot easier to complete). But one cannot stray too far from the 'correct', and circumscribed, path. One can, in the main, only perform actions that have been predicted or allowed for by the game-fiction's designers. For all that Lara Croft is presented as a species of archaeologist, for example, the possibility of capturing the Tyrannosaurus rex, or even photographing it, is not allowed within the terms of the game. *Tomb Raider*'s realism does not cater for many of the eccentricities of human behaviour, nor allow Lara Croft to engage in much irrelevant activity. This protagonist never sits down and starts singing in the middle of a quest. Nor does she sleep, eat, defecate, or (disappointingly enough for Lucozade) often feel the need for an energy drink.

To dismiss *Tomb Raider*'s fictional credentials as a result of its basic linearity of progression, for the apparent limitation of freedom of action, or even because of its violent approach to problem solving, however, would be to miss the implications of an alternative, and literary, line of descent that might be traced for this kind of game-fiction. We should recognise not just the extent to which J. R. R. Tolkien and his imitators inspired so many of the fantasy role-playing and text-based adventures that came before *Tomb Raider*, but the root source of so much of that fiction that is to be found within the folk tale form. And it is through an examination of the points of correspondence with, and deviation from, the formal characteristics of the folk tale, particularly as they are expressed within quest narratives, that we can begin to see a new form of storytelling emerge in *Tomb Raider*.[6]

In many ways *Tomb Raider* conforms to the generic conventions of the folk tale, and particularly the quest narrative, and wears many of its folk tale credentials on its sleeve. Lara Croft may not be a Jack, or even a Jill, but she has much in common with the princely heroes of many quest narratives. She is, after all, an orphan of aristocratic stock, the daughter (so the basic back-story to the games to be found in the manuals informs us) of Lord Croft. She lives in the contemporary equivalent of a castle, even if her mansion has a swimming pool rather than a moat. In several of the games in the series she 'starts' from this point (it is the equivalent of *Tomb Raider: The Last Revelation*'s Angkor Wat training level in both *Tomb Raider II* and *III*), before moving on to an extended quest which might be broken down into a series of smaller folk tale quest narratives or plot fragments. Despite the more or less contemporary trappings of the *Tomb Raider* series (usually to be found in things you can shoot things with, or things you can drive) and its otherwise unstable 'historical' locations (a distinctly contemporary Area 51, what looks like a near future/post apocalypse

London, and a 'primitive' island society of indeterminate location in time within *Tomb Raider III* alone), the *Tomb Raider* series has one foot firmly situated in the land of folk tale.

Strange beasts walk abroad, dragons stir in their lairs, and every 'tomb raiding' expedition is presented as quest rather than housebreaking and petty larceny. As in *Tomb Raider* there are few extraneous or irrelevant encounters within the folk tale quest narrative: anyone or anything encountered will prove to be either an adversary or a helper. Overcoming adversaries through violence is virtually mandatory and, as in *Tomb Raider* or any amount of contemporary *Rambo*esque versions of the quest narrative, there is no ethical or moral problem with such violence. Like the overcome adversaries of the quest narrative, the corpses that should litter the landscape of *Tomb Raider* simply fade from the story, and the screen, and disappear. The occasional riddle must be solved. Often an object must be retrieved (as in the quest for the Holy Grail, or in the inverted quest to dispose of Tolkien's One Ring). The unstable 'anytime' setting of *Tomb Raider* carries an echo of the 'Once upon a time …' invitation to listen, or read, of the folk tale.

The satisfaction of such stories, at least at the level of the discrete plot fragment, rests not in matters of plot sophistication, but in matters of the sophistication of telling. The question is never *will* the prince overcome the dragon but *how* will the prince overcome the dragon? Once the player has recognised the obstacle at hand (a dragon), and quite possibly failed to react in the appropriate manner (you die: the story is badly told), he or she might simply reload the game from the last point at which it was saved and attempt the moment of telling again and again until satisfied (you live: the story is told properly). What larger plot there is is irrelevant. As such the player of the game is engaged in the creation of a form of fiction at variance from conventional or written tellings. The game-fiction is no more 'authorless' than any other form of fiction, but this is the most 'writable' of texts, with the player/reader actively engaged in the construction and telling, and not just the reception and decoding, of the tale.

Nor is Lara Croft exactly the same kind of invincible hero that one finds in either quest narratives or action movies. In *Tomb Raider* we 'care' about this protagonist enough to keep reading the text because of her fallibility and her fragility. Action heroes and the heroes of quests do not die (it is a central given of the genres), and yet the movie-maker or storyteller must constantly place the hero in a position of tension where death appears to be a possibility. The player, however, is 'only human', works with the expectations of the action hero or quest narrative genres (the hero *should not* die), is aware of a tension that exceeds that available within film or prose narrative (the hero *might* die), and can only achieve the satisfactory closure of the plot fragment by conforming to readerly expectations (the hero *does not* die). Apparent responsibility for whether this particular Tinkerbell 'lives' or 'dies' rests, as with the conceit of J. M. Barrie's stage production of *Peter Pan*, with the audience. A degree of authorial responsibility is also passed to the reader in the possibility that the story might be told in a clumsy manner (the protagonist suffers damage, runs into walls, falls off a ledge, the player is forced to use medical packs to heal a wounded protagonist etc.), or as Lara Croft is manoeuvred with fluid grace as she jumps and rolls and shoots, this story may be very well told indeed. Along with the normal readerly pleasures of advancing the larger plot and finding out what happens next, the reader of game-fiction can share in some of the pleasures of the creation of the well-turned phrase or the elegant sentence as the boundary between reader and author becomes blurred.

Another area where the *Tomb Raider* quest narrative differs from the formal workings of its oral or literary antecedents is in the limited illusion of freedom of choice offered that works against the expectations of linearity. Options might be restricted to the essentially prosaic 'Which weapon shall I use?', 'Shall I pause to pick up the object on the floor?', or 'Which exit shall I leave by?', but the illusion of choice exists, and for all the third-person gameplay of *Tomb Raider* this places the emphasis on the first-person control available. It might even be argued that the authorship of 'good' game-fiction of this type (in terms of readerly satisfaction) depends on getting the balance right between that illusion of choice (leaving the telling to the player) and the appropriate placement of enough clear markers of plot progression for the player to find and so move on (a matter of authorship). However sumptuous the visuals and however gorgeous the rendition of the backgrounds, it would be a strange individual indeed who is satisfied with endlessly wandering around a level from which all adversaries have been eliminated, all levers pulled and all blocks pushed.

The plot-markers that are encountered, then, inform the player or reader of the type of story to be told. The player then undertakes the telling of this small-scale story and is rewarded by being able to advance to the next plot-marker, and sometimes with a near-cinematic vignette such as the Venice canals sequence in *Tomb Raider II* discussed earlier in this chapter. The game also provides a number of methods of gauging just how good a reader and/or teller the player is. Like the aristocrats of popular imagination, Lara Croft never carries cash with her, and the game's alternative capital (that can be both hoarded and spent) comes in the form of the flares, medical packs, ammunition, and objects that are acquired and 'spent' as the game progresses. The excess that the player sustains provides a measure of success. In addition, the game contains numerous 'secret' areas (often referred to as 'Easter Eggs') that are a little off the beaten track or difficult to access. That many of the secrets are hardly secrets at all, and might be blundered into without intent, hardly matters. It is possible to make progress within the game, and even to complete it, without gaining access to any such secrets, and so their acquisition is another method of keeping score, and another indicator of the player's ability as reader. It is as if a novel contained areas of sub-plot that were cordoned off from the main body of the narrative, and accessible only to those readers who somehow prove their sophistication of reading. An analogy might be found, perhaps, in the intertextual play of some contemporary fiction where recognition of an authorial reference to something outside the novel (a play, another novel, a film, a song, a political speech etc.) adds a further element to the readerly experience. But the seamless integration of the secrets of *Tomb Raider* into the major narrative, and their democratic accessibility (one does not have to be familiar with the entirety of world literature, music, cinema, or politics to access these secrets) makes them of a different order entirely.

There may be little opportunity for Lara Croft to engage in truly irrelevant action, but *Tomb Raider*'s designers have embedded some irrelevance into combinations of movements that almost amount to a variant form of secret. The first time that Lara Croft performs a graceful handstand or swallow-dive, moves not described in the manuals and likely to have emerged out of an accidental combination of key strokes, the player might be impressed as well as surprised. The availability of such actions, and the presence of secret areas that 'we' discover where 'lesser' players might miss them makes this, potentially, an almost competitive form of text. But, as in life, there is little point in having access to a secret if one cannot share it with someone else. It is more or less commonly accepted that the consumption of other cultural products (again, I am thinking primarily of film, television, and novels) is not an entirely solitary experience. As the flourishing of readers' groups for the discussion of literature in contemporary Britain indicates, the reading of novels generates a desire to share one's understanding with others, and the massive expansion of available television channels has only reduced, but not eliminated, the workplace or social post-mortem of the following day. No visit to the cinema in company is complete without a sharing of impressions. And so it is with the computer game, where discussion of what one has found that others might have missed, or the discussion of where one has become 'stuck' is the meat and drink of conversation in the playground, the workplace, the letters pages of games magazines, and (increasingly) in the chatrooms of the Internet. It is in this communication of not only what is necessary to complete a particular game-fiction, but also what it is possible to achieve within any game-fiction, that one can detect the most radical departure of game-fiction from other fictional forms.

Beating the system

What has been discussed up to this point might best be described as the conformist reading or playing of a game-fiction like *Tomb Raider*. The linearity of the game's essential structure and the limitations of possible movements are respected by the 'ideal reader' posited so far. It is possible to imagine a more or less perfect reading of the game, with all secrets discovered, all items picked up, and the journey undertaken from beginning to end at speed. We can also throw in a few handstands and swallow-dives for the sake of elegance. The illusion of many possible outcomes, that will be stressed as a potentially positive characteristic of game-fiction throughout this volume, however, would encounter the negative closure of the singular.

Indeed, descriptions of such 'perfect readings' are published by the games manufacturers themselves, in computer games magazines, and on Internet 'walkthrough' sites. Manufacturers and publishers have also been known to squeeze a little extra profit from the need for such perfect readings if you are to be able to complete many games. As Rex the dinosaur is shocked to discover when he stumbles across a commercial walkthrough in a toy store in *Toy Story 2*, the solution to a game is often inaccessible from within the game itself, and the player is forced to buy a second product. Even leaving aside the similar feelings of betrayal as trusting player or reader that the need for such secondary texts inspires, the commercially available walkthroughs expose the mechanistic bare bones of the game's structure. What follows is a fairly typical example taken from a magazine walkthrough for *Tomb Raider III* published in February 1999:

> Go around the corner and quickly kill the dog and thug before entering the doorway in the centre. Stand on the weak floor to the right to fall through. Pull the block towards you and then climb out. Drop down the other side and follow the path along and climb out to the right. Go to the end and around the corner. Here you'll find two switches to the right.[7]

And so on. In some ways it is as if a novel arrived in a box in which are to be found a jumble of sentences on small slips of paper. Context, and an awareness of the kind of novel that we are attempting to read (through the cover illustration, the blurb, the content of individual prose fragments, and the presence of a few introductory paragraphs), would allow the piecing together of some passages according to authorial design, but there would be inevitable false turns and wrong steps. Only with the purchase of an addendum that mapped out the correct order for the piecing together of text could one be confident that the reader had read the novel 'properly'. It is unlikely that such a novel would attract a large readership. This is not Dadaist poetry or the cut-up texts of William Burroughs, where the random juxtaposition of prose fragments produces the aesthetic product: one is always reminded that a coherent structure exists within the game-fiction, and that the inability to read correctly (most dramatically illustrated by the 'death' of the protagonist) is a consequence of a failing of reading.

The presence of the 'save game' option, and its frequent use by players, indicates a recognition that it is common to read 'badly', at least in the short term, and that to do so indicates something other than 'illiteracy'. A failure of reading that is not quickly resolved results in frustration as there is a collapse into unreadability, and the player of a commercial game-fiction is more likely to blame faulty authorship than his or her own reading ability. The presence of 'cheats' that allow the player to skip forwards in text or acquire a full inventory of weapons and accessories are, as their name implied, an unsatisfactory intervention that similarly indicates a failing of reading.

A perfect reading and playing through of even such a technically accomplished game as *Tomb Raider*, if accomplished in one sitting and captured and then replayed on video, perhaps, would make for a rather long and tiresome computer-animated film of fairly low quality. The extent to which *Tomb Raider* was a mechanistic authored narrative that channelled the reader through the basic binary options of 'correct' and 'incorrect' choices would be blatantly apparent, and the computer game would appear to be unable to lift itself out of the ghetto in which it is confined as an immature and inferior form of visual entertainment whose only feature of passing interest would be the sense in which the text can only be activated 'correctly' by a reader who demonstrates sufficient 'skill'.

A rather different vision of the possibilities of game-fictions emerges, however, once we consider the existence of a different kind of reader who does not merely conform to, but transgresses, the limitations of the authored (and authorised) narrative. The realism of *Tomb Raider* is, as already noted, a stylised visual illusionism, and yet it displays an internal coherence that adds equivalents of physical laws (only certain doors can be jemmied open with the crowbar, only certain blocks may be pushed or climbed, for example) to simulations of physical laws (gravity points 'down', there are limitations on how fast one can sprint, how far one can jump). The resemblance of the game landscape as a recognisable simulation of a real world, its visual realism, allows common sense to govern gameplay (falling on spikes hurts; one cannot walk on water; if you are on fire, diving into water will (probably) extinguish the blaze) that further establishes limits. Within the game one must always be aware of such laws and apply such common sense, just as one must always be aware that deviations from the linear progression of the game are only temporary, and at some point one must move on in the 'correct' fashion. Must, that is, unless this is one of this second type of posited reader of game-fiction, what might be termed the 'subversive reader'.

The subversive reader is also likely to be, or to have been, the ideal reader already discussed. He or she will be well aware of how one 'should' complete the game, but will deliberately reject any notion that this is the only way the game-fiction can be read or played. Such a reader works within the internal logic of the game-world to evade the limitations imposed by the 'legitimate' authors (level designers and programmers) to engage in a little 'illegitimate' authorship himself or herself. Such potentially subversive activity can range from the relatively minor (taking the pacifist option, for example, and refusing to draw guns on any opponent) to the extreme (the exploitation of programming errors, or 'bugs', to short-circuit the linear plan laid down by the game designers). The new possible emplotments (interestingly entitled the 'expert's challenge' on at least one *Tomb Raider* site) are often posted as additions to Internet walkthroughs. There is no other form of fiction where the subversion of authorial design allows for the retention of a coherent narrative and has become a common form of reading.

A little such subversion, of course, is actively encouraged by the design of some levels, indicating the recognition of the producer that an element of open-endedness and an extension of the illusion of freedom of action might be as important to the success of the game as its strong drive through a clearly linear emplotment. One such moment when *Tomb Raider*'s designers have obviously moved to accommodate the more subversive impulses of their audience can be found in Lara Croft's mansion home in *Tomb Raider II*. The Croft mansion is used as a training level in several of the *Tomb Raider* games, and variously features an assault course, a swimming pool, and a gym in which players can familiarise themselves with the basic game moves. The house and grounds can also be explored, and the basics of puzzle solving and button-pushing are introduced. The house is also free of any other animate presence except for a butler controlled by the game's artificial intelligence (unless one counts the use of the mansion as a final climactic level following the 'false ending' of *Tomb Raider II*). For all that the frail and elderly butler, who follows the player's moves around the mansion carrying a rattling tray of tea things, might be a gentle dig at transatlantic expectations of how an 'authentic' British aristocrat might live, he is also an irritant. His persistent shadowing of the player's progress, and the obstacle he presents to movement as he doggedly attempts to present tea to the lady of the house, prove frustrating to many players. In the training level of *Tomb Raider II* Lara Croft does not have access to any weapons, so the standard (and unsubtle) method of dealing with a 'problem' is not available. The solution to this particular 'servant problem' however, is not particularly difficult to work out. Move Lara Croft to the kitchens, open the door to the walk-in meat locker and enter. Wait for the butler to bring in his tea tray. Leave rapidly and press the button to close the door. Problem solved.

This differs from the usual run of *Tomb Raider* gameplay in several significant ways. The mansion exists outside of the major game-plot, and is a space in which there is no imperative, or even opportunity, to 'progress'. There is no absolute need to dispose of the butler. The player is not necessarily following the 'correct' course by locking him in the meat locker, and even in this largely amoral game-world it is possible that to do so is to indulge oneself in the childishly subversively enjoyment of the 'incorrect' in locking a frail old man in a refrigerator while one goes out to play. But there is another undeniable satisfaction of player as reader at the discovery of what amounts to another 'secret' sub-plot. It is another sign of the sophistication and expertise of one's reading, and the absence of the imperative (I have completed a story fragment because I *can*, not because I *must*) adds to readerly satisfaction.

That players would attempt to circumvent the butler could hardly have come as a surprise to the game's designers. In the target-range addition to the assault course in *Tomb Raider III* they even work with the expectations of player abuse of the butler in having him wear targets on his front and back, and he suffers the indignity of being knocked down again and again by his employer as she practices her gunplay. But such moments within the game of excess and surplus, whether deliberately 'authored' or not, mark a departure from other forms of fiction. The realism of the *Tomb Raider* game environment may be limited and circumscribed, but once within its fictional frame the player can act in ways the programmers and designers could not have foreseen.

There is something undeniably satisfying, for example, about gaining access to an area of the game landscape that the designers obviously had not prepared for, if only to be treated to the sight of areas of missing backdrop or a collapse of the illusion of three dimensions and solidity. Similarly, finding ways of taking vehicles into areas that the designers had not predicted generates a certain subversive pleasure. Such pleasures are necessarily short-term, however, because of their almost inevitable detachment from the linear progression to which a player will have to return. It is only the relative inaccessibility of such areas, and the feeling that one is confounding authorial intention rather than meekly submitting to it, that makes them of interest rather than a source of frustration.

What is striking is that the game-fiction does not necessarily collapse into meaninglessness when the player or reader attempts to subvert authorial design. Recognition of the limitations of *Tomb Raider*'s essentially linear emplotment, particularly that individual episodes or levels are entered and exited, usually, through single points, does not prevent the subversive reader from tearing up the 'intended' plot and constructing his or her own narrative. If we return to consideration of the Venice level of *Tomb Raider II*, we can begin to see how this works. The player enters the canals area from a specific point in a motorboat, and even a little exploration identifies the single exit point – a firmly closed gate protected by underwater mines. As the player explores further, the doors and gates that must be opened, levers pulled and opponents that must be shot all make themselves known in one way or another. The presence of a 'spare' motorboat offers a hint as to how to dispose of the mines that bar the exit. The allusions made to the Bond films in the Venice levels, with their exotic 'holiday destination' setting, ominous 'Mr Big', henchmen in suits, and the presence of a fast boat in a landscape in which there is some suspiciously ramp-shaped architecture, all point to the intended grand finale already described.

The subversive reader will not be ignorant of the plot markers that are tugging at his or her consciousness, and will usually be able to complete the level as ideal reader, but will also be aware that it is possible to attempt to read or tell this story fragment in a different way. The most basic of progressive plots is obvious: I have entered by point A, and must leave by point B. What one does at points in between, however, is open to readerly intervention. One might miss out on the full visual spectacular of the sub-Bond cinematic finale if one finds a way of swimming out of the level, rather than taking the speedboat route, but one has access to the pleasure of subversion. One might be making things far more difficult for oneself if one refuses to engage with all the henchmen and dogs that patrol the level, but one has rejected authorial dictat and exercised a form of readerly freedom. It is in this exploitation of the game-fiction's realism to write a variant narrative that the interaction between reader and text foreground the more radical possibilities of this as a form of fiction. *Tomb Raider* might, as yet, be limited in the freedom of action and open-endedness it consciously allows, or produces without intent, but its players and readers have already recognised, and exploited, the ability that this form of game-fiction allows to subvert the clear distinction between the act of reading and the act of authorship.

Notes

1 The full implications of any sense of possible 'immersion' in the computer game are dealt with at length in Chapter 3 in relation to *Half-Life*.
2 This is not true of sloppy programming, rather than the conventions

of representation established throughout the series. *Tomb Raider*'s first five outings have all been accused, to a greater or lesser extent, of being 'unfinished', with a tendency for Lara Croft to be able to move her limbs through apparently solid objects such as walls and doors. While it is easy to see why so many players find this frustrating, it can also contribute to the pleasures of subversive reading I discuss in the final section of this chapter.

3 See Catherine Belsey, *Critical Practice* (London: Methuen, 1980). Belsey's account of the 'classic realist text' of nineteenth-century fiction sets out as a significant corrective to some of the misunderstandings that accompany literary realism.

4 The standard literary-critical term for such fictions that self-consciously foreground their fictionality is 'metafiction'. See Patricia Waugh, *Metafiction: The Theory and Practice of Self-Conscious Fiction* (London: Methuen, 1984). Rushdie, Marquez and Carter have sometimes been grouped together under the apparently tautological title of 'magical realism' that does not necessarily so much inform as suppress recognition of the variety and difference on display within the works themselves.

5 This walkthrough was originally to be found at www.tomraiders.com (accessed September 2001), a site now no longer operational. Another site that provides a similar walkthrough can be found at www.azerista.com/tombraider/wthtrlr–2.php (accessed November 2002).

6 Making such a move at this point in my study inevitably allows me to introduce those basic approaches to narrative that are usually referred to as structuralist (focusing on the structure of the text), and form the intellectual base of narratological approaches to texts. What follows essentially emerges from that body of work pioneered by Vladimir Propp in *Morphology of the Folk Tale*, trans. Laurence Scott (Austin, TX: University of Texas Press, 1968). See also Tsvetlan Todorov, *The Poetics of Prose* (Oxford: Blackwell, 1977).

7 Unsigned article (1999), '*Tomb Raider III*: Full solution', *Ultimate PC* 19, 132–51, 140.

3

Gritty realism: reading *Half-Life*

Half-Life [inc. *Half-Life* (1998), *Half-Life: Opposing Force* (1999), *Half-Life: Blue Shift* (2001)]. First-person shooter. The player controls the actions of an in-game protagonist from a first-person perspective. What the player sees is what the protagonist would see. Progression through the game largely involves forward movement through a series of areas within a government research complex. There is a limited need to interact with objects and the landscape. All versions of the game offer variations on a basic escape and evasion theme, with protagonists attempting escape from both human and alien opponents after a scientific experiment goes badly wrong. Occasional excursions are made into an alien dimension. The three versions of *Half-Life* offer three varying perspectives on events: those of Gordon Freeman, a scientist involved in the experiment, Adrian Shepherd, a member of a military team sent in response to events, and Barney Calhoun, a security guard.

Any notion that game-fictions such as *Half-Life* and *Tomb Raider* might point, however vaguely, towards the eventual development of an increasingly refined form of computer-based fictional text would appear to be extreme if one were simply to judge them according to the sophistication of the stories that they tell. While this study does not seek to minimise the extent to which fictions such as *Half-Life* are essentially formulaic, it is how they are told and how they are read that concerns us here far more than the content of their stories. In this sense we are more concerned with the possibilities for the future of narrative telling implied in *Half-Life* than with what it actually achieves. Admittedly, the plots currently on offer in most game-fictions are, like the dialogue they contain, particularly open to criticism for being primitive, juvenile, and often almost painfully crude. Not only do many game-fictions rely on an extensive audience understanding of the conventions of a wide range of popular genre fictions in order to function as readable texts, they also currently demand that their readership be content with fictions that (as games) are extremely limited in their textual ambition even when compared with other forms of popular genre fiction.

That *Half-Life* is 'only a game' and yet manages to present any kind of involved emplotment at all has been seen as something of an achievement. To some extent an acknowledgement of the more obvious limitations of the form are part of an unspoken and tacit agreement between player and text to make fewer demands of game-fictions than of films or novels – no one expects great dialogue in a game-fiction; no one looks for depth of characterisation; no one judges the success of a game fiction on the sophistication of its back-story or the logic of its scientific extrapolation. A parallel might even be drawn between the current state of audience expectation of this nascent form and that experienced by the audience of early cinema. In the early twenty-first century it is still possible to gather a paying audience for a game-fiction on the promise of the presentation of previously unseen spectacle, as it was when films of train wrecks played to satisfied audiences in the early twentieth century. Technological advance allows the presentation of ever more impressive visual spectacles that paper over the cracks of a lack of sophistication in other areas. Particularly in the case of weaponry, something that looks good on screen is far more likely to be included than something that emerges from the strict application of physical laws or narrative logic. Narrative consistency often becomes subservient to the demands of the promise of spectacle, and is little more than a way of moving from one big bang to the next. As the producers of the film version of *Lara Croft: Tomb Raider* (2001) have discovered to their cost, contemporary cinema audiences can be far less forgiving.

Story, such as it is, more often than not provides a wafer-thin narrative excuse for the real meat and drink of such game-fictions – shooting things to impressive effect. Sometimes cut scenes and FMV sequences have been used effectively to present a developing story, as in the rather arch video-casts and news broadcasts that had linked missions in Westwood's *Command & Conquer* series of real-time strategy games, but often their essentially mechanical function is all too visible. In *Command & Conquer: Tiberium Sun* Westwood managed to entertain in its often camp rendering of the unfolding conflict between the Global Defense Initiative (the clean-shaven square-jawed 'good guys') and the Brotherhood of Nod (the quasi-terrorist 'bad guys' with a convenient habit of wearing black), but the role such cut-scenes served for setting the victory conditions which had to be met if the game is to be won remained barely concealed. It is also worth noting that it is usually possible to dispose of such narrative links with one or two keystrokes, which indicates just how peripheral they are to the core business of gameplay.

Half-Life goes beyond the conventional model of presenting a sequence of linked mission briefings to offer what appears to be an organically developing plot as often 'explained' through what is overheard as through what is told directly to the protagonist, but such explanatory statements are still a potentially interesting addendum to the unfolding of the game rather than a necessary part of gameplay. The plot that unfolds through the combination of audio and visual discovery (essentially that Freeman has been betrayed and lied to) is interesting enough in its cumulative effect, but it hardly demands that the reader be alert to the subtlety of possible meanings or any potential for any ambiguity of meaning. It can be assumed that everything we are told is a falsehood. We would be in error, however, if we make too many assumptions about there being any imperative for the imparting of information about plot development (even in the form of a series of untruths) through language. *Half-Life* prioritises vision over language, and constructs a world in which 'seeing is believing'. Should the audio speakers fail while we are playing *Half-Life* it is the absence of non-linguistic cues that might indicate the location and nature of a threat that would be the greatest loss to the game – not the loss of the words spoken by the game's other characters. What this chapter shows is that *Half-Life* makes different demands on its readers than many of the games that preceded it, demands that require a refinement of our understanding of how game-fictions might communicate their meanings and construct narrative without any dependence on the mediation of language.

Before *Half-Life* is discussed in detail, however, it is worth giving brief consideration to some of the negative press that game-fictions have received. This demotion of the importance of language as no longer the primary system of signification in game-fiction arguably compounds the simplistic classification of game-fictions as inevitably crude, and unable to provide a challenging reading experience. At the risk of caricaturing the negative reception that game-fictions have often encountered, the reading of the written word is socially valorised as it demonstrates a skill, 'literacy', that is accepted as an unqualified 'good'. The development of an equivalent ability to 'read' game-fictions is taken as a given, something that, like an ability to read television, demands no equivalent skill level and can be achieved by the pre-literate or the illiterate. It therefore appears to belong firmly outside supposedly 'high' culture, accessible to children and those lacking in the kind of education that has traditionally been seen as providing access to art. As any reader who is older than their late teens will be able to confirm, the challenge of *Half-Life* is more to manual dexterity and hand-eye co-ordination than to what are often thought of as the 'higher' brain functions. The puzzles that are supposed to be so taxing to the thinking processes of your average games player are often little more than variants on the theme of 'square peg through square hole', and are hardly comparable with the complex textual decoding activities of the reader of, for example, the detective novel. There is even a possible connection between the continual need to use one's finger to trace out a reading of a game-fiction (although there is no parallel need to move one's lips) and the vague contempt in which it is often held. At first glance everything about *Half-Life* conspires to confirm just how 'low' it is in relation to the high culture versus low culture debates that continue to inform discussions about the 'value' of texts.

Textual content also fixes game-fictions at the lower end of such a scale of assumed textual value. In terms of overarching plot, both *Tomb Raider* and *Half-Life* are essentially heroic adventures apparently inviting the most basic form of identification ('and with one mighty bound *I* was free') that are as notable for their political naivete and ideological conservatism as they are for their technological achievement in presenting detailed worlds on screen. It is possible, for example, to see many of the individual episodes in *Tomb Raider* as providing a remarkably consistent metaphor for a kind of (British) imperialism that is, understandably, only rarely celebrated in contemporary culture, and only rarely offered up at all without accompanying critique. The aristocratic Lara Croft travels to foreign climes armed to the teeth and filled with the kind of spirit of adventure that would have made Rider Haggard proud and still been familiar to Ian Fleming as he drafted the earliest of the James Bond volumes. Foreign space is full of traps and snares, and the threat that it represents is only defused through violence and (often) through the application of superior technology. Those representatives of the various indigenous populations that are not to be dealt with violently are regarded as significant only in so far as they have temporary use-value. Even those individuals who aid Lara Croft, such as the local guide who lights her way in the opening 'Tomb of Set' sequence in *Tomb Raider: The Last Revelation*, are mute. 'Native' inhabitants have no pretence of independent subjectivity, and are usually little more than types taken off the shelf marked cultural cliché, whether they be spear-waving Polynesian tribesmen or staff-wielding Tibetan monks. Lara Croft's dismissive statement 'Egypt, nothing but pyramids and sand' in the film *Lara Croft: Tomb Raider* might be ironically presented, but it nevertheless reveals something telling about the ways in which the games, and the film, apprehend the 'other'. Indigenous cultures are only of real interest in terms of the commodity value of the artefacts returned to the colonising homeland. Like a latter day Lord Elgin, Lara Croft's primary interest is in the extraction of these artefacts for return 'home', although to the private gallery of the Croft estate rather than to some digital version of the British Museum.

Half-Life is a much more internal and American affair, but is no less guilty of offering up a fictional world from which the political, moral and ethical complications of the adult world, and even much of the popular fiction read by adults, have been excluded. The violence of *Half-Life*, and this is an exceptionally violent game in which most player control is given over to the aiming and firing of a wide range of weapons, is never sanitised as it is in *Tomb Raider*, and it can never be forgotten that at the centre of the camera view of the first-person perspective are the cross-hairs of a gunsight. There is no question that the only way one survives under threat is to be armed, and not to hesitate in using weapons. There is an occasional need to take a finger off the fire button so that the protagonist might seek help from some of the cowering scientists who are also trapped within the Black Mesa complex, and a degree of cooperation with other characters is required within *Opposing Force*, but this is driven by self-interest (kill a scientist, soldier or guard needed to open a crucial doorway and the game terminates) rather than an accommodation of humane motives. Recognition of the 'other', be it human or alien, is more often than not simply the prelude to its destruction. That process of 'othering' is even made explicit in the lack of obvious humanity in many of the game's opponents – not just in the form of the alien entities, but in presenting the special forces troops that hunt down Freeman as faceless behind their gas masks.

This game does demand serious and careful consideration as a work of popular fiction, however, and the observation that *Half-Life* owes much of the feel of its interface to combat flight simulators (that similarly place a gunsight centre-screen) discussed in detail at the end of this chapter should not blind us to the obvious lack of simulatory intent. If *Half-Life* is simulating something, then it is not simulating lived experience. Although its visual reference is largely to a possible near-future, its emplotment gestures far more firmly towards the 1950s science fiction B-movie and its big-budget descendants than to the real world. Those elements of the real that are used as reference markers are often disturbing. An essentially off the shelf B-movie alien invasion plot is combined with the kind of paranoid anti-government fantasies that inform the thinking of US 'militiamen'. But they combine to provide the twin frames of xenophobic fear of the alien other coming from without and the persecution of the individual from within by shady government men in suits carrying briefcases. This is a basic dramatic premise that has become a contemporary fictional staple, perhaps best exemplified by Chris Carter's *X-Files* series. Freeman is the quintessential figure of American self-reliant individualism, gun-toting and capable, but he remains a fictional type, a contemporary Hawkeye or Dirty Harry, rather than a meaningful representative of the survivalists holed up in the wilds of Montana.

Unlike some other games that have foregrounded their reference to the real (counterterrorist games such as *Rainbow-Six* (1998), or small-unit games such as *Hidden and Dangerous* (1999)), *Half-Life* has always been clear in communicating its fictionality. It might be accessible to the illiterate, at least as far as literacy is classically defined, but it demands a different kind of literacy within the codes and conventions of popular culture if it is to make meaningful sense as an extended text rather than a sequence of unconnected fragments in which all one does is move the gunsight and press the fire button. *Half-Life* acts to guarantee that the violence that is at the heart of the game is internally justified as a response to the world of the text, and that the visual allusions made to other works of fiction act in some way to protect it from the kinds of critique that would be encountered by a more 'serious' work of art. There are plenty of visual markers that declare loudly that this is 'only a game', and a game that makes knowing reference to a range of popular genres that themselves are rarely taken seriously (primarily the science fiction B-movie and the genre horror film). To be too po-faced in response to its violence, or its ideological conservatism, is to invite the automatic defence offered up by so much of contemporary popular culture – that one is missing the irony, has failed to note the knowing nudge and wink, and should approach the text on its own terms.

And yet *Half-Life* has been seen as setting something of a benchmark in game-fiction history, setting a gold standard of both 'storytelling' and 'realism' that subsequent game-fictions have been measured against. The game's developers have certainly foregrounded this aspect of the experience, as the following promotional text taken from the publisher's website demonstrates:

> Throughout the game, both friends and foes behave in sophisticated and unpredictable ways, a result of Half-Life's powerful and innovative artificial intelligence. The intensity of the game also reflects the strong storyline, created by award-winning horror novelist Marc Laidlaw.[1]

The naming of an author is still a relatively unusual move within the promotion of game-fictions, and it is worth noting because what we have here is the central tension between a scripted fiction sourced in a human author and the lack of 'predictability' introduced through the operation of a 'sophisticated' artificial intelligence.[2] Somewhere in the intersection of the 'authored' (and therefore 'predictable') and the 'unpredictable', *Half-Life* manages to offer a reading experience that is of a different quality from that which was offered by its competitors in the late 1990s. This chapter seeks not so much to support the more hyperbolic claims for *Half-*

Life's radicalism as a groundbreaking text, as looking at the mechanics of its storytelling processes to interrogate the ways in which it works as a supposedly interactive form of text that makes the most of this point of intersection. *Half-Life* is offered as an example of 'first-person' game-fictions through which some of the more extreme claims for the future of game-fictions – that they represent something through which it is increasingly possible to see the elision of the distinction between simulation and real – can be evaluated in a critical manner.

Welcome to Black Mesa

Survival, and not exploration, is the core principle that drives *Half-Life* forward. After an extended opening sequence that familiarises the player with the in-game environment and establishes the sense of workaday normality from which *Half-Life* will subsequently deviate, visual curiosity plays second fiddle to an often justified paranoia. *Half-Life* has its own basic puzzle sequences that must be solved and switches that have to be thrown in the correct sequence, but it rarely allows the kind of aimless wandering about that had so characterised the larger exterior or cavern levels of *Tomb Raider*. Such touristic moments of restful admiration of the static game landscape as those that accompany Lara Croft's meanderings are few and far between within the unforgiving environment of the Black Mesa government research complex in which most of *Half-Life* is set. The game's designers have gone out of their way to make this a frenetic, rather than leisurely, form of entertainment where even the most mundane of contemporary environments, the corporate office, takes on a terrifying potential. Every ceiling tile, every ventilation duct, every wall recess, every corner, and every pool of radioactive sludge represent potential sites of ambush. Even apparently empty stretches of corridor where alien entities can 'spawn' in a burst of electrical discharge are the possible locations of an encounter that will end the reading experience of *Half-Life* abruptly, and in a terminal fashion. The helicopter gunships and alien entities of *Half-Life* are undeniably impressive if one fixes the in-game camera in place long enough to take in the detail with which they have been rendered, but they are more likely to pose a direct (and brief) threat than to be present simply to amaze and astound. The player of *Half-Life* has to learn quickly not just to 'look', but to 'look out'.

Until the text moves into the 'other dimension' from which the aliens have come, the visual quality of the landscape is far more 'gritty' than that provided in most of *Tomb Raider*'s locales. Even when there is time to stop and look, this landscape is remarkably mundane, grimy and soiled. Only in the dystopian future London of *Tomb Raider III*, with its mutant commuters and wrecked Tube stations, does *Tomb Raider* approach the intensity of disintegration and offer a similarly 'infected' humanity to that of *Half-Life*. What looks like a decommissioned Cold War missile site is already falling into decay, rust-streaked and stained when first encountered by the player. This is a landscape of rivets and iron plate, where the miniaturisation of technology and the development of plastics has had little impact. There are no futuristic i-Macs or evidence of contemporary ergonomic design in these offices. Interior colours are muted, light sources are infrequent, and areas of deep shadow are the norm. Noxious chemicals are spilled in pools in the corridors, containers of toxic waste are scattered about, and corpses litter the floor. Any expectation that emerging from underground will provide much relief are also disappointed – when not resembling military car parks the exteriors are most often ledges carved out of canyons that are static and lifeless. Even before the alien incursion that damages so much of the infrastructure, the solid state hardware of Black Mesa is in disrepair. Lights flicker, the electrics play up, doors jam. When the game is played from the point of view of the security guard Barney Calhoun in the third episode in the series, *Blue Shift*, colleagues encountered on the way to his post complain about the alarm system, and the moment of release from his own introductory train journey into the complex establishes the extent to which this is a site of malfunctioning technology rather than a techno-fetishist's dream of utopian potential. The first doorway Barney attempts to open fails to recognise his pass and has to be opened by a guard on the other side. In a moment that exemplifies the kind of internal reference which has since proved so appealing to the dedicated fan-base that *Half-Life* has acquired, the frustrated Barney can also be glimpsed hammering on this door as Gordon Freeman makes his own initial journey into the bowels of Black Mesa.

This pervasive air of future decay, of course, is familiar enough from genre science fiction texts, be they Golden Age or cyberpunk. Yes this is the future, with all the technological trappings and advanced hardware of an extrapolated future society, but the most basic message conveyed by the physical manifestations of that future is one of scientific and technological failure. Perhaps surprisingly in a text dependent on technology for its very existence, both technology and science are almost literally demonised here – or at least they are made responsible for conjuring the demonic, as the careless meddling of men in lab-coats results in the invasion of alien entities. Science opens Pandora's box and it is only individual human agency (in actions taken by Freeman and therefore by the player or reader) that saves mankind.[3] Such a move invites obvious readings as an expression of the kinds of anti-scientific distrust now all too familiar as scientific intervention in the 'natural world', such as the genetic modification of food or the potentials of cloning technologies that fail to convince a sceptical public of their benefits. We might have survived the Cold War and the fear of imminent nuclear annihilation that had informed so much science fiction of the 1950s and 60s, but we have our own contemporary anxieties expressed through our popular fiction. In a characteristic reduction of a complex issue to a clear binary opposition between good and evil, we quickly learn again how foolish it is to meddle with things we do not understand. Playing about with 'anomalous materials' in *Half-Life* opens some sort of interdimensional gateway that allows in invading aliens – taking up a gun and acting with extreme violence allows the individual to solve the problem in a rather direct fashion.

What amounts to a gritty engagement with contemporary cultural anxieties is also reflected in the effect that the protagonist can have on the in-game landscape. To offer a quick gloss on some of the jargon that has emerged in relation to game-fictions, *Half-Life*'s 'deformable environment' (that is, its landscape that can be affected by the actions of the player) is part of a basic strategy of 'immersion' (the conceit that one might somehow 'forget' that one is playing because there is no collapse into illogical lack of cause and effect).[4] Immersion, when successfully achieved, allows the reader to remain 'in' that environment because attention is not drawn to the surface of the screen that actually intervenes between reader and text. In *Half-Life* the player remains within a landscape marked by the consequences of his or her actions, and one is not even allowed to ignore the consequences of the violence that is so necessary to progress forward. In *Tomb Raider* the corpses of the dead fade quickly from sight leaving only possible pickups to mark the point of their passing. We are left with medi-packs or piles of ammunition, and not with pools of blood or the bodies of the slain. Within Black Mesa there is some attempt to place pickups at logical points such as lockers or armouries (although the frequency of crates that may or may not contain useful items when broken open is already a tired cliché of first-person fictions as narrative logic clashes with the necessities of progression through the game), and in *Half-Life* rather gory reminders of the carnage that is wreaked litter the landscape. To be too offended, however, by the cartoon representation of spilled internal organs, lumps of meat and fragments of bone might well be excessive. This may be gore, but it is cartoon gore that depends for its effect, and distances itself from any possibility of being truly disturbing, by its location within the 'buckets of blood' school of visual representation where excess neutralises its potential to shock.

That this aspect of the visual experience can be disabled as 'inappropriate for younger players' indicates its status as peripheral to gameplay in a manner that does not apply to the more damaging effects the player can have on the physical landscape. Except in very rare, and scripted, instances whatever one does with some fairly heavy weaponry in *Tomb Raider* has no lasting effect on the game landscape. For those with the inclination in *Half-Life*, large chunks of scenery can be destroyed with heavy weapons, and it is even possible to draw crude images on walls through a combination of carefully aimed gunshots. The *Half-Life* manual describes such possibilities almost exclusively in terms of 'realism':

> Half-Life's environments are as realistic as possible, and this level of realism will affect the way you move around. For instance, there's gravity – if you stand on ceiling tiles, don't be surprised if they collapse under your weight. There are also multiple surface effects – yes, wet floors really are slippery. And, if hit hard enough, glass will break.

Of course, the claims that can sometimes be made for such a deformable landscape (as contributory to the establishment of a form of realism) are a little disingenuous. One might, conceivably, mark one's progress through sometimes confusingly similar corridor sections by leaving a mark on walls, but the ability to do such damage appeals to a far more primal urge in most players. In a sense *Half-Life* allows a level of irrelevant action and even mindless stupidity that is deliberately excluded from a game such as *Tomb Raider*. The advice offered in the manual for using heavy fixed weapons in *Opposing Force*, for example, encourages excess by pointing out that there is no danger of running out of ammunition, and suggests that if 'you encounter a mounted gun, try firing it at every solid structure in sight'. This is not just advice relating to game play, where the landscape needs to be destroyed in order to allow progression, but amounts to an encouragement to wreak the kind of havoc that can have an undeniably impressive visual effect. Again, as when the player is given full control of the Black Mesa monorail carriage, the game's designers have taken note of how much an audience still enjoys the sight of a good train wreck.

On a much smaller scale, if you attempt to use the crowbar that can be acquired in parts of the *Tomb Raider* series all that will happen, unless the protagonist is positioned at an appropriate point, is that we will be treated to a rather stern 'no' from Lara Croft. In *Half-Life* the crowbar can be used to mark surfaces, smash computer screens, break open all crates (and not just the significant ones that might be levered open by Lara Croft) and otherwise vandalise an already distressed environment. No one tells the player off in *Half-Life*, no matter what he or she chooses to do. As it also says in the *Opposing Force* manual, 'If it's stupid but works, it isn't stupid.' The claims for consequent immersion in the lack of prescription of possible action, however, are perhaps extreme. There is something related here to that most basic contractual agreement between reader and text that Coleridge, discussing his 'supernatural' contributions to *The Lyrical Ballads*, referred to as 'the willed suspension of disbelief for the moment'.[5] There are fewer reminders that suspension of disbelief is an act of will, and fewer collapses into a lack of cause and effect, than had been previously characteristic of most game-fictions that constantly brought our attention to the surface of the text–reader interface as we were forced to realise that the fictional world without 'surface effects' and equivalents to physical laws just didn't 'make sense'. But as such this is a matter of intensity rather than a radical departure. The ability to 'effect' the environment that is so proudly foregrounded is essentially limited to being able to inflict damage upon it, rather than to have truly multiple choice. When Freeman is faced with a lovingly modelled drinks vending machine the options available to the reader are revealingly limited. Hitting the 'action' or 'use' key does not result in the orderly purchase of a fizzy drink. Do the cabinet some serious damage with crowbar or firearm, however, and drinks cans come tumbling out. Black Mesa might come equipped with all the necessary facilities for the fulfilment of basic human bodily functions, with its vending machines, staff canteens, toilets, and shower cubicles, but the possibility of engagement in any everyday human activity (beyond the initial commute to work) is, as in *Tomb Raider*, extremely limited.

A potentially more interesting attempt at the construction of a supposedly immersive environment is apparent in the handling of sound, and shows that *Half-Life* has learned the lessons of recent horror films that have also depended on what might be termed an audio 'grittiness'. As *The Blair Witch Project* (1999) had demonstrated so effectively to much of its audience, low visual quality, a first-person perspective, and a soundtrack of unexplained noises off can be combined with great effect within the horror genre. Music, of a kind, still plays as we move through the text, but in place of the kind of rousing orchestral accompaniment that had provided a backdrop for Lara Croft's more impressive entrances and exits, or the explicit musical cues that had alerted the player to imminent danger, the soundtrack of *Half-Life* features scuttling movements, strange screams and wails, the crackle of electrical shorting, and the grinding and crunching of machinery. Nor should the visual and aural realism of *Half*-Life be dismissed out of hand because it is real*ism* and not real. Like the best genre horror movies, *Half-Life* is genuinely capable of generating convincing fear responses in its players. It can, in a way that *Tomb Raider* is rarely able to do, make its players 'jump'. *Half-Life* is described here as gritty in its realism at least in part to distinguish it from the limited operation of an internal logic in *Tomb Raider*, and to take account of this focus, always, on a sustained illusion of an internally consistent world that is closer to experienced reality than anything offered in the *Tomb Raider* series. The level of *Tomb Raider*'s aural realism, in comparison, is probably best indicated in the quasi-orgasmic sighs produced when Lara Croft is inadvertently run into walls. As a text that makes much use of the paranoid delusions of conspiracy theorists (the government is not to be trusted; aliens will invade at any moment) as well as some perhaps more compre-hensible, if extreme, workings through of contemporary anxieties ('science' is meddling with things it does not fully understand, with possibly disastrous consequences) *Half-Life* provides a constant series of aural reminders that 'they' really are always 'out to get you' that never break the illusion of immersion.

This general grittiness of intent and effect spills over into the manner in which the game is played out. Where a successful reading encounter with *Tomb Raider* can concentrate, as noted in Chapter 2, on the construction of a visually pleasing series of po-tentially graceful movements, often within set-pieces that are in some ways analogous to cinematic experience, there is a far clearer sense of urgency in *Half-Life*, where the emphasis is less upon the achievement of grace and more upon the handling of a form of pressure that is generated through the continual possibility of in-game 'death'. Exploration of an often stunning visual environment plays its part in *Half-Life*, particularly when Freeman or Shepherd enter the alien dimension, but the aesthetic qualities of the visuals in the main body of the game are secondary in function to their status as possible threats to the safety of the protagonist. As such it represents a very different kind of fictional text to that already dis-cussed, one where the very ability to engage in the equivalent of turning the page, rather than the appreciation of how stylishly one is constructing a reading experience, is dominant, and in which the skills of reading that are prioritised are far more related to speed of recognition allowing for an immediacy of reaction than to any sense of nuance or elegance.

The potentially subversive reader of *Half-Life* certainly has fewer opportunities to exercise her or his subversive tendencies than in *Tomb Raider*. In its very restrictions form, at least, also echoes content. Freeman, Calhoun and Shepherd are trapped, and it is a basic and deliberate irony of naming in the first episode of *Half-Life* that Freeman is anything but free – confined within what amounts to a physical entombment in the lower levels of Black

Mesa, confined within genre, and confined by a progressive emplotment that allows little deviation. The movement from one plot fragment to another is relentlessly linear, opportunities for digression or deviation are comparatively limited in a game set mostly in corridors with single entrances and exits, and there is a real attempt to generate a sense of urgency in relation to time through the constant expectation that one will not be 'allowed' to continue in unbroken sequence. Pause for breath or contemplation within *Half-Life*, and all too often the opposition will come to you. If you hesitate after being spotted, then small alien entities (that bear more than a passing resemblance to the 'face-hugger' stage of the eponymous alien in the *Alien* film franchise) scuttle forwards, or special forces troops rush towards Freeman and throw grenades. Constant engagement with the game is required, and the act of reading is one of perpetual activity if one is not to have any illusion of immersion broken. To stay within the frame of the game for as long as possible, to not be expelled from it to the management screens as a consequence of in-game 'death', is as much a part of *Half-Life* as it was for players of arcade cabinet versions of *Space Invaders* (1978) or *Asteroids* (1979), whose eyes were never allowed to lift from the screen or fingers move from the control buttons. The player might not have to return to the very beginning of the game after such an expulsion, or have to insert more loose change, but the process of reading is disrupted, and any illusion of immersion in the game environment is dispelled.

To draw negative conclusions from this structural linearity, however, (to conclude that *Half-Life* represents little more than a graphically sophisticated arcade experience, for example) seems to suggest that there is little that is new here, beyond the technology of delivery and the refinement of the visual experience. In terms of formal characteristics one might as well be using the computing potential on one's desktop to play *Space Invaders*, or even solitaire – as so many Microsoft Windows users still do. We turn the cards, follow the rules, and when we lose we begin again. Check an option box on the solitaire game in Windows and you can even keep score. If there is something new in game fictions such as *Half-Life*, then it is not to be found in the confinement of its linearity, or in its inexorable formal movement from level to level of increasing difficulty. Its departure from solitaire, or other game fiction forms where screen after screen of marching green blocks had to be eliminated, rests in its handling of notions of how this story is constructed not through an incremental increase in score from level to level, or through a reliance on a telling of plot through language, but on a reading of largely non-linguistic cues that nevertheless combine to construct a narrative that will be unique to each reader. This construction of a unique text only comes about through a variation on the standard contract that reader has with text – a contract that depends on the promise of readerly freedom if the player acts within the internal logic of the text.

With the absence of Lara Croft's 'no' in *Half-Life* comes the realisation that the game's mechanics are grounded in a desire to liberate the player even as he or she attempts to liberate Freeman. We really are not going to be 'told' what we can or cannot do. One might even draw on one of the most basic distinctions of narratological analysis, that between 'showing' and 'telling', to establish what it is about *Half-Life*'s attempt at immersion that has seen it so lauded for its originality and has placed the confinement of its thematics and its mechanics of gameplay in stark relief against what amounts to a species of liberation within storytelling. This liberation within storytelling then allows us to apply all our will to the suspension of our disbelief, and always for just a little while longer. The definitions of 'showing' and 'telling' offered by Shlomith Rimmon-Kenan remain useful in establishing the implications of these terms:

> 'Showing' is the supposedly direct presentation of events and conversations, the narrator seeming to disappear (as in drama) and the reader being left to draw his own conclusions from what he 'sees' and 'hears'. 'Telling', on the other hand, is a presentation

mediated by the narrator who, instead of directly and dramatically exhibiting events and conversations, talks about them, sums up, etc.[6]

As a primarily visual form, like most drama or film, the game-fiction inevitably prioritises showing over telling, but it is the extent of that prioritisation within *Half-Life*, and its consequences, that we need to be alert to here. The very extent to which 'telling' is subordinated allows for the illusion of readerly freedom to be constructed, and an apparent liberation to be had from the tyranny of the prescriptive narrator who would condition meaning.

And this would appear to be the key to *Half-Life*'s achievement. In a game where the freedom of the individual to act is always under threat, the mechanics of the game concentrate on this handing over of individual responsibility from other representatives of authority (Valve's development team; the named author Marc Laidlaw) to the reader. *Half-Life* might be formulaic, but within the constraints of its formula an illusion of individual agency is constructed. To borrow another element of Rimmon-Kenan's work (that owes much to Brian McHale and originally related to matters of speech representation within prose fiction) when thinking through these strategic moves made in relation to showing and telling it is possible to draw an imaginary axis with *diegesis* (in this context defined as an obvious act of telling) at one end and *mimesis* (an obvious act of showing) at the other. Telling is an essentially diegetic strategy, and showing a mimetic strategy, and the further one is from diegesis and the closer one is to an act of mimesis, the more the text appears to be handing over this interpretative responsibility to the reader. As Wayne Booth had noticed as early as 1961, the making of such a distinction between 'showing' and 'telling' also involves the making of value judgements about the texts that we read: 'Much of our scholarly and critical work of the highest seriousness has, in fact, employed this same dialectical opposition between artful showing and moralistic, merely rhetorical telling.'[7] Despite Booth's implication of negativity in his reference to 'merely rhetorical telling', this distinction is not finally reducible to a simple classification of 'showing equals good' and 'telling equals bad', but the most significant effect of a concentration on showing over telling is to move a game-fiction like *Half-Life* further along our imaginary mimetic axis than a game-fiction like *Tomb Raider*. What is argued throughout the rest of this chapter is that it is the distance that *Half-Life* has travelled along this axis, the extent to which mimesis is approached, that has resulted in the plaudits of its critics and the readerly satisfaction of its audience.

Valve's own claims for the storytelling aspect of *Half-Life* are certainly demanding of further consideration in this context: 'Half-Life combines great storytelling in the tradition of Stephen King with intense action and advanced technology to create a frighteningly realistic world where players need to think smart to survive.'[8] On the one hand there is a clear appeal here to the 'tradition' of popular genre fiction exemplified, in sales terms at least, in the work of Stephen King. On the other hand the 'great storytelling' is only one element in this mix – 'action' and 'advanced technology' combine with storytelling to create this world. What we have here is a recognition of a difference between 'story' (the linked events) and 'narration' (the how of the communication of those events). Narration emerges out of the tripartite human–text–machine interface where there is a physical encounter with technology, and cannot be simply fixed solely in some exterior figure of a narrator, but in the reader who also functions as narrator. The artificial intelligence might be unpredictable, but it responds *both* to the already written script, *and* to the actions of the reader. In effect, the player or reader of *Half-Life* is telling himself or herself the story in a fashion that is inevitably unique to that individual, and to that moment, and the lack of predictability guarantees an individual and unique experience. As such the game-fiction is able to offer up a form of mimesis more or less unavailable in other forms of popular entertainment. It is noted often enough that life does not have the organisation of art, and yet the game-fiction offers up apparent disorganisation (it is closer to lived experience, is more 'realistic', or at least more mimetic) while nevertheless remaining readable in a satisfying way.

In such a context, the title of *Half-Life* itself bears examination not only as a potential reference to textual content (science plus danger) within a term that describes the decay rate of radioactive isotopes, but for what it might reveal about the self-consciousness of this attempt at mimesis. Rather than being simply descriptive, 'half-life' might even be a potentially useful mediating term that may be of some use in classifying the degree and form of realism attained by itself and other comparable examples of game-fiction – this is emphatically *not* life, but is *half*-life, a representational approximation of 'life' fully aware of its limitations (as an attempt at mimesis), rather than something that represents a fractional attainment of 'life' that implies eventual realisation of its potential for simulation in a confusion between text and real.[9] Should it ever go too far towards the absolute simulation of life, as is argued in detail in the final section of this chapter, it would fail as readable text. It is the recognition of limits, as well as its attempt to push those limits, that is the major achievement of this as readable fiction. To place such emphasis on a possible distinction between 'mimesis' over 'realism' is not just a matter of logic-chopping or of semantics: as new forms of text and representation have emerged alongside the personal computer, so an accompanying language has entered common usage that is not always subject to clear definition, and the offhand and casual usage of 'realism' needs more careful consideration than has been currently recognised. In much the same way that the term 'virtual reality' does not mean 'virtually' real in the sense of approaching the real in any imminent and meaningful way, but instead refers to a representational technological construct that is *other than* the real, so the 'realism' claimed for *Half-Life* offers something that is clear in its representational status.

The extended opening sequence of the original episode of *Half-Life* provides a clear example of the ways in which this particular game-fiction experience negotiates the competing demands of the need for the unseen hand of the game's authors to retain narratorial control of what is possible (that risks alerting the player to the fact that suspension of disbelief, or immersion, is an act of will) and the desire to hand over apparent narratorial control to the reader (that runs the risk of forcing the game into unplayability). Running at just under five minutes on even a high specification computer, this sequence not only indicates the recognition of the debt owed by *Half-Life* to film conventions, but indicates the extent to which it is prepared to go beyond the limits of film's fixed point of view. There is a comparable mix of plot establishment, information delivery, and technical display as is found in the cut-scenes and FMV sequences of *Tomb Raider* in this opening sequence. To an extent the reader is a similarly passive recipient of a carefully planned visual experience as (in the manner of cinema) the credit sequences roll as a printed overlay on screen. The point of view of the player is moved inexorably forward as a light railway carriage travels on a monorail through Black Mesa. A certain amount of 'telling' is offered up as a calm voice-over provides further information about the facility, its safety rules, and its basic procedures. The length of this initial journey serves not only to familiarise the first-time player with the visual style of the game landscape, but emphasises the extent of the entrapment and entombment from which the reader will have to escape, with a sequence of heavy doors sealing behind him or her as the journey is made ever deeper into the facility.

But it is important to note that *Half-Life* departs from the clear distinction between gameplay sequences and FMV sequences that was a such a formal feature of *Tomb Raider*. *Half-Life* offers a (limited) visual mobility throughout this initial journey that goes far beyond normal cinematic experience. The protagonist can be manipulated around the interior of the railway carriage to allow the player/reader a more extended look at the various personnel going about their daily business, the arc-welding robots, automated transports, missile silos, or helicopter gunships that provide the more interesting distractions throughout the journey. This ability to have a degree of apparent control over the visual spectacle is an example of the integration of all aspects of *Half-Life* within a consistent visual register. In the opening sequence of *Tomb Raider II* the player was presented with a carefully choreographed sequence showing a journey to the Great Wall of China by helicopter that was not only presented as a passive experience, but was of a different, and superior, visual quality from that of the body of the game-fiction: in *Half-Life* there is no similar hierarchy of visual quality. Once the game-world of *Half-Life* is entered it offers an internal consistency. We might not be able to experience the same kind of subversive pleasures of reading available to the player of *Tomb Raider*, but we are given the possibility of engaging in a plural reading experience in exercising choices of observation, and of taking a readerly responsibility for the detail of textual progression.

A clear sense of urgency is added to this transfer of narrative authority, and is established through an unforgiving approach to the possibility of failing to read well – the protagonist of *Half-Life*, whether Gordon Freeman, Adrian Shepherd or Barney Calhoun *will* 'die'. To 'fail' in one's reading in *Half-Life*, and to fall repeatedly into the ultimate (if not 'final') confinement of 'death', is not only possible – it is more or less inevitable. The fragility of the protagonist, the expectation that in extreme circumstances the human frame will not be able to survive, however, is hardly a gesture towards realism in a world where one can heal the protagonist by plugging him into one of the helpful first-aid machines mounted on the walls. The first of 'Murphy's Combat Laws' listed in the manual for *Opposing Force* is 'You are not a superman' – a point implied, perhaps, in the naming of a Gordon, an Adrian and a Barney in the three episodes of *Half-Life*. But the likelihood that you will 'die' really functions to point up the degree of continuing readerly responsibility for authorial function that is part of what is termed here the contract of reading *Half-Life*. Unlike *Tomb Raider*,

where that contract had demanded the discovery of correct sequences of pre-scripted actions, the emphasis, here, is far less on
the elegance with which progress is made through the plot, but on
the very possibility of any progress being made at all.

The imminence of the possibility of failure is, perhaps,
signalled in the way in which the save game options are handled
differently in each of these game fictions. There is an expectation
built into *Half-Life* that the reading experience will, again and again,
be brought to an abrupt halt by the 'death' of the protagonist. It is
also important to note what we are actually saving – we save a point
in narrative progression: we do not save Freeman. The game auto-
matically saves with surprising frequency, and the player can 'quick
save' with a single keystroke that does not demand expulsion to
the management screens. Unlike other fictional forms, where the
reader or viewer reads with the full knowledge that the protagonist
will survive and the pleasure of the text results from the unfolding
of the 'how', rather than the resolution of the 'whether or not', there
is something different happening here, and something that foregrounds the extent to which reading is an active, and not passive,
occupation.

I am a camera

Half-Life belongs to a specific sub-genre of game-fictions, the 'first-
person shooter', that, as the presence of an option to lower the level
of gory detail might indicate, has the potential to provoke an understandable degree of public disquiet. Nor is this merely a matter
of trying to protect the impressionable young from images that
might disturb. The concentration on notions of 'first person' involvement ('I' act, rather than 'Lara Croft' acts, for example) appears to be at least partially responsible for such disquiet. In
addition, common use of the identifier 'shooter', the term used by
police forces in the United States to describe the perpetrator of
armed crime, raises the spectre of there being some connection
between those who play games belonging to this genre and those

who commit acts of actual violence. In a world where, as Jean Baudrillard predicted, simulation threatens the distinction between true/not true, the simulation of the actions of the lone gunman for the purposes of entertainment, and particularly for the entertainment of the young, inevitably raises questions of taste, and in some quarters, of decency. Such texts appear to present themselves as something other than texts – something to be 'acted out' rather than something to be 'read', where the success of that act of performance is judged not by audience consensus or the level of applause that greets the fall of the final curtain, but by body count. Realism, a term rarely used with any critical sophistication in the marketing of such games (and yet a term that all marketing teams continue to deploy with enthusiasm), becomes a stick to beat the genre with in such circumstances, particularly in the immediate wake of specific tragedies involving firearms where the search for root causes and causal explanations is at its most intense. At the very least the strident claims for realism made by games developers and publishers seem to allow a confusion to exist between actions taken in the world and engagement with the world of the game-fiction – which it is imperative that we recognise as an act of reading.

It is worth noting that this confusion is even more extreme in the case of game-fictions than it is in those other areas of popular culture that have the portrayal of extreme violence at their core. Cinema disarms criticism of its portrayal of violence in a number of obvious ways, whether it is the aestheticisation of the excessive within approximately contemporaneous films such as *The Matrix* (1999) or *Crouching Tiger, Hidden Dragon* (2000), or the placing of violent excess within a humorous frame, as in so many contemporary action movies. Similar strategic moves made by the designers of game-fictions, and *Half-Life* makes extensive use of both strategies, seem to carry less weight when the player/reader is understood to not only 'watch' but to somehow 'enact' that violence. What this study seeks to address here is what is considered to be the error of regarding a game-fiction such as this as an act of simulation rather than mimesis. The same technology can be used to simulate (and a number of armed forces are reported to use one-shot, one-kill, first-person shooter games to train their members, and flight simulators are routinely used to train both civilian and military pilots), but this is not what we encounter when we read *Half-Life*.

Half-Life stands out among the examples of the first-person shooter produced in the late 1990s in a number of significant ways, both because of its careful incorporation of those cinematic strategies that function to disarm the unease generated by the portrayal of violence, and in its consequent emphasis upon the realisation that this is a fiction, and should be read as such. 'It's OK to shoot things,' it exclaims, 'because this isn't real life, it's *Half-Life*. It's a paranoid-science-fiction-conspiracy-theory-thriller-horror game.' Its illusion of independent agency is just that, and *Half-Life* succeeds as a game-fiction precisely because it is not simply attempting to simulate the aiming and firing of weapons in the most 'realistic' fashion possible, but to involve the reader in a consciously recognisable act of reading. This form of game-fiction might have grown out of, and continue to be related to, those computer simulators that attempt to present a plausible analogue of experience, but it does not constitute an unproblematic simulation itself, and any understanding that the reader of *Half-Life* might somehow mistake simulation for real is misinformed.

It is far easier to find examples of such confusion in fictions that consider the far future, rather than in the current generation of game-fictions themselves. As Iain M. Banks has noted, for example, in his 'Culture' novel, *Look to Windward*:

> The dozen or so civilisations which would eventually go on to form the Culture had, during their separate ages of scarcity, spent vast fortunes to make virtual reality as palpably real and dismissibly virtual as possible ... Thanks largely to all this pre-existing effort, the level of accuracy and believability exhibited as a matter of course by the virtual environments available on

demand to any Culture citizen had been raised to such a pitch that it had long been necessary – at the most profoundly saturative level of manufactured-environment manipulation – to introduce synthetic cues into the experience just to remind the subject that what appeared to be real really wasn't.[10]

It is essential to note just how far the distance is that remains between the visual environment shown on screen in contemporary game-fictions and the real world. The possibility for confusion addressed through the introduction of 'synthetic cues' in the virtual reality environments in Banks's Culture is simply not a problem faced by *Half-Life*, as even a cursory glance at a screen when the game is running will confirm. However high we set the screen definition, we need no reminders, even in terms of visual quality that 'what appeared to be real really wasn't.'

It will be a long while before designers of fictions such as *Half-Life* have to go to the lengths of the Culture in alerting their audience to the fictionality of their product. Even those futuristic explorations of the potential for confusion in the human encounter with the machine have pointed up the lack of likelihood for any real confusion even when it will (perhaps) be allowed by the technology. When the crew of the starship *USS Enterprise* enter the holodeck in the television series *Star Trek: The Next Generation* (1987–94), for example, the audience might be forgiven for thinking that they are being shown the eventual consequences of the development of first-person viewpoint game-fictions such as *Half-Life*. Gone, apparently, is the mediating presence of a Lara Croft analogue as individuals are inserted directly and seamlessly into a fictional world. The distinction between what is real and what is computer generated is certainly blurred in *Star Trek*, at least from the point of view of the crew member in question, as he or she moves around a computer generated space indistinguishable from other space, interacting with computer generated characters equipped with such a sophisticated level of artificial intelligence that their dialogue is indistinguishable from that of the crew. In part this is the result of the removal of any physical interface – in this hologramatic future there is no screen providing a barrier as well as access to the fictional, no keyboard, joystick or mouse to manipulate, no clumsy virtual reality glove or helmet to remind the individual of the artificiality of the experience.

Despite what might be expected to be the final achievement of the promise of realism within such an experience, that depends on the direct manipulation of normal sensory input without the need for any prosthetic aids, however, this remains an excursion into other fictional alternatives. At times, and in the finest tradition of the original *Star Trek* television series, where parallel evolution saw some suspiciously historical versions of planet Earth scattered throughout the universe, these episodes also have the character of the small child allowed to play in the dressing up box, or at least let loose in a studio costume department as intensive play is made with the conventions (and costumes) of a wide range of film and television genres. That all this occurs within the frame of a television programme in which many of the other 'real' elements are provided through the intervention of computer graphics, of course, allows for a near flattening of difference between *Star Trek*'s vision of the real and *Star Trek*'s vision of fantasy. That the crew member experiences a three dimensional hologramatic representation has to be taken on trust, as the viewers' access is filtered through the two dimensions of the television screen. Special effects are no longer so 'special', but are instead a necessary and more or less constant element in the visual mix available to genre science fiction in both television and film. And, necessarily, there is no actual difference between the quality of a visual event that takes place in the holo-deck and a visual event that takes place in other spaces within the *Star Trek* universe.

Nor is this interest in a blurring of distinction between what is real and what is artificial unique to Iain Banks or the producers of *Star Trek: The Next Generation*. In many of its manifestations it seems to allow dramatic tension, and even paranoia, to be

constructed from this very inability (always posited some time in
the future) to distinguish between the real and the fictional. When
Philip K. Dick's short story 'We can remember it for you wholesale'
was adapted for the big screen as *Total Recall* (1990), for example,
the inability to distinguish between real event and artificial event
placed directly in memory was central to its plot. Even the *X-Files*
(1993–) has made play with the negative potential of such confusion in updating the plot of Michael Crichton's *West World* (1973)
in an episode co-written by William Gibson and entitled *First Person Shooter* in which real deaths occur within a fictional space where
players take part in a game that itself owes much to multiplayer
computer games such as *Quake Arena* or *Counter-Strike*, the
multiplayer arena version of *Half-Life*. In written fiction, the example of Gibson's *Neuromancer*, in which the essentially
recognisable artificiality and geometric abstraction of cyberspace
is accompanied by potentially more interesting sections in which
the main protagonist is caught in a simulation indistinguishable
from lived experience, has been followed by many imitators.[11] In
each case, what is at stake is the very life of the reader, with the
possibility of real rather than in-game 'death' marking out the future game-fiction as potentially lethal, rather than simply able to
corrupt the young.

The good news, at least as the technology of delivery stands
at the very beginning of the twenty-first century, is that such confusion between real and fiction is impossible to sustain within computer game-fictions themselves, even as the ambition of its
approximation is in some senses at the heart of the first-person
game experience. Such elision and flattening is possible on the big
screen, on television, or on the page because of a lack of visual
difference between the representation of the computer generated
simulation and the representation of the real. In *Half-Life* that move
towards the visual accuracy of representation is far more related to
the contribution it can make to the provision of originality of spectacle (it is 'better' than what has gone before because it is 'more

realistic') than to any desire to deceive. After all, I cannot be alone in thinking that 'I' would respond to experience of the events that occur in Black Mesa in a somewhat different fashion than 'I' do when I adopt the role of Gordon Freeman. The crew of the *Enterprise* might suspend their critical judgement of what is or is not real, and the artificial memories of *Total Recall*'s Doug Quaid might be presented as of such fine resolution that he is temporarily unable to distinguish between what was lived and what was placed directly into memory, but the player of *Half-Life* is in little danger of such confusion.

Freeman is not simply a vehicle through which the reader might insert himself or herself into this fictional world. The reader is more than likely in conversation to refer to Freeman's actions in the first person ('… and then I rounded the bend in the corridor and the ceiling fell in on me …') but he and Shepherd and Calhoun remain roles to be played. Identification, such as it is, is not absolute or unproblematic. The mediation of their fictional presence might not be visible in the same way that Lara Croft remains visible at all times, but it always intervenes to reconfirm that we are reading text and not acting in the world.

Notes

1 http://sierrastudios.com/games/half-life (accessed September 2001).

2 This is beginning to change, both in frequency and in the reference not just to an author who is accepted as proficient outside the world of the computer game (as an 'award winning' writer of genre horror fiction, for example), but in the naming of games designers as 'authors'. The most obvious current examples are Peter Molyneux, named in all the marketing material for *Black & White*, and Sid Meier, whose name routinely precedes the titles of the games he produces, such as *Sid Meier's Alpha Centauri*.

3 A discussion of 'agency', and its relationship to narration is provided in Cohan and Shires, *Telling Stories*, pp. 83–112. The specific section dealing with narrating agency (pp. 89–94) will be particularly useful for anyone wanting to trace the ways in which narratological theory

has integrated what is essentially a sociological term.

4 The problematics of any celebratory understanding of immersion that situates the reader as the passive consumer of the computer game product is touched on briefly by Scott McCracken in *Pulp: Reading Popular Fiction* (Manchester: Manchester University Press, 1998), p. 118, when discussing Julian Stallybrass, 'Just Gaming: Allegory and Economy in Computer Games', *New Left Review*, 198 (March/April 1993), pp. 83–106.

5 Samuel Taylor Coleridge, *Biographia Literaria: Biographical Sketches of my Literary Life and Opinions*, in James Engell and W. Jackson Bate (eds), *Collected Writings of Samuel Taylor Coleridge VII* (Princeton, NJ: Princeton University Press, 1983), vol. 2, p. 6.

6 Shlomith Rimmon-Kenan, *Narrative Fiction: Contemporary Poetics* (London: Routledge, 1983), p. 107.

7 Wayne Booth, *The Rhetoric of Fiction* (Harmondsworth: Penguin, 1961), p. 61.

8 www.valvesoftware.com/projects.htm (accessed November 2000).

9 Nor is this a coincidence of naming unique to *Half-Life*. The more recent first-person shooter *Unreal* (1998) makes much of the level of simulatory visual 'realism' that it provides, but in its title shows how this realistic excess is tempered by a strident demand for recognition of its fictional status as a game.

10 Iain M. Banks, *Look to Windward* (London: Orbit, 2000), pp. 350–1. This novel centres around exploration of a culture in which the 'save' option is available to all, and looks at the impact that such a possibility would have on the way we live, and the way we would then approach death.

11 A useful account of 'cyberspace' that both recognises the limits of current technology and offers up a succinct reading of *Neuromancer*, can be found in Adam Roberts, *Science Fiction* (London: Routledge, 2000), pp. 167–80.

4 Replaying history: reading *Close Combat*

Close Combat [inc. *Close Combat* (1996), *Close Combat II: A Bridge Too Far* (1997), *Close Combat III: The Russian Front* (1998), *Close Combat IV: The Battle of the Bulge* (1999), *Close Combat: Invasion Normandy* (2000)]. Real-time strategy/wargame. As the titles indicate, various episodes are set in different military campaigns during the Second World War. The game is split between the strategic management of large formations on campaign maps and the tactical control (in 'real-time') of small numbers of troops on battlefield maps. At the strategic level the player controls options that may include resupply, reinforcement, the allocation of air and artillery support, and the movement of large units. At a tactical level the player controls a small number of units indirectly through the issuing of a limited range of defend, move, and fire orders which may or may not be carried out by the units on the ground. All versions of the game are playable as single and unrelated battles, or in a campaign mode that allows the construction of an extended narrative following several weeks, or even years, of conflict.

Of all the game-fictions selected as primary examples in this study, *Close Combat* is the least likely to be an instantly recognisable brand name even to those who spend their leisure time staring at a computer monitor. Its relative popularity as a games franchise might be indicated by the longevity of a series that had seen five episodes released by the year 2000, but it has hardly become a household name in the same way that *Half-Life*, *Tomb Raider*, or *SimCity* have. Its profile even among other real-time strategy games, itself an extremely popular sub-genre of game-fictions, is relatively slight.[1] The choice of *Close Combat* as an example, rather than a more typical example of a real-time strategy game such as *Command & Conquer* or one of its imitators, however, is due to its crossing of genre boundaries – this is a real-time strategy game, but it also has ambitions of historical representation. As an unashamed wargame, that foregrounds the accuracy of its reference to historically verifiable data, it undoubtedly appeals to a comparatively niche market when compared to games such as *Half-Life* or *Tomb Raider*, or even *Command & Conquer*. As noted in Chapter 1, this particular niche has its own problems of negative public perception that limits the size of its potential audience, but *Close Combat* also goes out of its way not to emphasise the extent to which it is 'only a game', but the degree to which it offers some kind of access to historical event through something its producers describe as 'realism'.

To consider *Close Combat* adequately we need to acknowledge its range of relationships: to the wargame, to narrative history, and to the un-narrativised historical event. Somewhere in the collision of these relationships, and at the moment of reading, a variant form of historical narrative is created that displays a potential unique to game-fiction. In its historical reference *Close Combat* makes the most of the erosion of the clear distinction between fact and fiction that continues to inform much contemporary critical and cultural theory. At the risk of falling into the kind of theoretical abstraction declared all too tempting in Chapter 1, it is worth noting that the potential redundancy of this distinction has caught the attention of many critics and theorists, including Paul de Man: 'The binary opposition between fiction and fact is no longer relevant: in any differential system, it is the space *between* the entities that matters.'[2] It is the new move that *Close Combat* makes within the 'space between' in game-fictions that is highlighted in this chapter.

In order to promote itself to a potential audience that will make historical as well as fictional demands of the text (not just how 'good a read' is this text, but how 'accurate' is it? Does the 'fiction' reflect the 'fact'?) it has consistently played on its seriousness and rejected the most obvious indicators of the game-fiction's playfulness in a way that none of the other games discussed so far have had to. In doing so it asserts both a level of scholarship that would not be out of place in more conventional historical works, and a firm relationship with historical data.[3] This chapter argues that the unprocessed historical field (where one might imagine that all the unnarrativised historical data from which written history is then composed is stored) is not just a toybox from which the game can borrow its playing pieces, but is shown what amounts to a duty of accuracy of representation by the games designers. This then places *Close Combat* in a position of intriguing tension in this 'space between' what is fact and what is fiction, and brings the question of what 'realism' might mean within historical game-fictions to the fore. This tension created between the fidelity it displays towards the historical field, and the liberties that are then taken with how a form of historical narrative may be constructed, can be seen to reflect wider changes in the way contemporary popular culture has approached questions of historical representation that need to be considered in some depth. Paul de Man, Hayden White, Dominic LaCapra, Linda Hutcheon and many others might have carefully mapped out the problematics of a simple fact/fiction distinction, but we still live in a world where the encounter of 'fiction' with 'history' is often read as a traumatic moment when written history is in danger of falling into 'falsehood' or 'deception'.

What this chapter explores with most interest are two distinct characteristics that can be found in a game such as *Close Combat*. Firstly we will look at it in relation to the more general sub-genre of game-fictions, the real-time strategy game, to which it belongs. Then we will consider it in terms of its reference to other historical texts that focus on matters military, and other texts sometimes labelled 'counterfactual' historical works. In looking at this game-fiction as a specifically historical text we concentrate on the ways in which *Close Combat* attempts to negotiate two ambitions that would seem to be incompatible with one another. On the one hand *Close Combat* attempts to address the desire for a level of scholarship comparable to that which informs the conventional historical work – it must be 'accurate', its attention to detail must satisfy an audience already likely to be conversant with the period in which it is set, its reference must always be to the historical record. On the other hand, this is not a narrative history or a historical documentary, it is a game-fiction. It depends on its ability not only to reflect or iterate historical detail from a supposedly 'objective' position (with its fixed distance reflecting that adopted by a certain type of military historian who concentrates on the details of the hardware over the human story), but for its most basic readability on its potential for departure from the historical record.

On the most basic level this can be expressed in short-hand form, and is primarily related to the playing of the game in its campaign mode – the starting conditions of the extended military campaign that is fought must begin from a moment of verifiable historical accuracy, but the reading experience within the individual battles that are played out must be one which allows, or even demands, divergence from the historical record. We must begin in something akin to the archive and end with a narrative story that may or may not tally with the historical record. The story that emerges cannot be compared to Leopold von Ranke's injunction to historians to 'show it how it really was', but might be thought of as historical in 'telling it how it might have been'.[4] I would not want to imply that *Close Combat* therefore has an educational potential as a means of delivering what are sometimes crassly termed the 'lessons of history', but I do feel that it puts this whole issue of how such historical texts might be read into question. In the process of examining how this particular 'space between' fact and fiction is exploited I will explore the possibility that this relates to wider contemporary debates surrounding the intersection between academic historiography and popular culture, debates that have seen the expression of anxieties about 'falsification' as much as about what is or is not 'appropriate' in the fictional work that would play games with history.

History in real-time

In Chapter 1 *Close Combat* was described as 'clean' in its removal of human suffering, tragedy, and distress, as well as matters of politics and economics, from its representational frame. We should not get too excited, perhaps, by the lack of potentially distressing human detail within such a game-fiction, or rebel too quickly against the glorification of combat that might be expected to emerge from such an abstraction. *Close Combat*'s claim is always to the 'space between', and never to the irrecoverable historical event. As a narrative text it emerges from the historical record, but does not claim to be anything but partial in what it represents. As such, its claim for historical veracity or realism is similar to that made by the military historian, rather than to those texts that attempt, from a position of personal experience or not, to capture the act of testimony or witnessing of the veteran. This does not pretend to be recovering historical 'truth', but to be telling a 'historical' story. Despite the frosty reception his essentially counter-intuitive thoughts received in some quarters, Jean Baudrillard had an important (and related) point to make in *The Gulf War Did Not Take Place*. When 'real' war appears to be indistinguishable from 'virtual' war we have cause for anxiety. As Baudrillard noted, 'The idea of a clean war, like that of a clean bomb or an intelligent missile, this whole war conceived as a technological extrapolation of the brain is a sure sign of madness.'[5] But the journey in the other direction goes nowhere significant – there is no comparable 'madness' in recognising an absence of real event beneath the visual images of *Close Combat*, only the sensible recognition of its fictionality. The delusion that Baudrillard protests against is the delusion that we mistake 'fact' for 'fiction', that we mistake war for videogame: in game-fictions like *Close Combat* we are never in any danger (at least in part because of this 'clean' representation of events stripped of all that inconvenient human detail that might turn the stomach of a television audience watching the nightly news with their dinners on their laps) of mistaking the videogame for real event.

When popular fiction that represents warfare is acknowledged to be serious in its historical ambition, rather than simply using history as a framework on which to hang gung-ho emplotments and the body parts of the 'bad-guys', it sometimes transcends its negative associations. Indeed, those popular fictions that have most closely approximated lived experience (so far – we should never forget the illusory potential of technology, after all), such as Steven Spielberg's *Saving Private Ryan*, or the television drama *Band of Brothers*, are commonly assumed to have possibly positive didactic effects, just as narrative history has. If nothing else, the opening minutes of the film act as a reconfirmation of the truism that 'war is hell'. It certainly acts to confirm our expectation that war is often an assault on the senses as well as an assault on the body. When Spielberg's attempt at authenticity and verisimilitude was reproduced in the first-person shooter *Medal of Honor: Allied Assault* (2002), with its own representation of the chaotic and confused storming of the Normandy beaches, the frequency of in-game death must have made the same simple point that allows the film to evade critique for suggesting that 'war is fun' – that there is something that is undeniably attractive in acting the historical voyeur at moments at which there is some consensus that human history is at a moment of 'crisis', but only a madman would see this as an attractive advertisement for actually being there on the day. To appreciate the excitement of the visual and aural spectacle of the war-film does not necessarily imply that the viewer might want to march down to the local recruiting office. Contemporary readers, even readers of Hollywood blockbusters and game-fictions, are more sophisticated than this.

If we have any concern that the accuracy of representation might somehow act the recruiting sergeant for those who crave such excitement, then it is worth noting again that even the first-person game-fiction is unable to sustain its own illusion of 'immersion'. We cannot even make the simplistic identification with the 'heroes' of the day that might be made by the viewer of *Saving*

Private Ryan or *Band of Brothers*. We 'die', again and again – they (or at least some of them) live to fight on in the second reel or the next episode.[6] *Close Combat* takes one step further back from any possibility of a thrilling illusion of immersion. Rather than concentrate on offering up the linked moments of exaggerated visual spectacle that feature in such fictions, *Close Combat* cultivates a largely sober text–reader interface that amounts to the self-denial of an unproblematic potential for entertainment. Both visual drama and possible actions are subject to restraint in a text that remains firmly fixed in its own textual 'half-life' or mediated position between fact and fiction, and will not allow the same kind of mindlessness that the player of *Half-Life* can engage in.

There is undeniably very little of the cartoon or the dramatic in the visual experience of *Close Combat*, and even in terms of the real-time strategy genre it represents something of a restrained experience that has been interpreted by some as a form of 'tedium' that makes this a sub-genre of little interest compared to the shoot-'em-ups and beat-'em-ups that proliferate on game consoles.[7] Its central military conflicts are concerned not with an equivalent of the knockabout battles between *Command & Conquer*'s GDI and Brotherhood of Nod, but between German and Allied units during the Second World War. Yes, this entertains, and one must presume that the fiercest advocate of *Saving Private Ryan*'s educational potential would accept that it too was an entertainment, but it never allows the player to ignore its relationship to that war. In making such clear and direct historical reference it inevitably has a more complex relationship with the real than its lack of reliance on visual illusionism might otherwise suggest. As the frequent use of archive footage reminds us, this was a real war in which real people died.[8] This is fiction, but it is historical fiction and carries some of the burdens of a need for verisimilitude that has long been a condition of this form of representation.[9] The pleasure offered by *Close Combat*, its success as historical fiction, is located in how it measures up as a 'realistic', or perhaps 'plausible' representation of historical event, as well as in how the story unfolds.

That the various episodes of *Close Combat* have as their subject military campaigns and operations that have also been the subject of big-budget big-screen treatments is no coincidence. The Normandy invasion (*Saving Private Ryan*, *The Longest Day* (1965)); Operation Market Garden (*A Bridge Too Far* (1967)); the invasion of Russia (*Cross of Iron* (1977), *Enemy at the Gates* (2001)); and the Ardennes offensive of 1944 (*The Battle of the Bulge* (1965)) have an inherent dramatic potential for this kind of telling. According to the received narrative recounting of the Second World War, all were high-stakes gambles, and only some of them paid off. They have been seen as moments of uncertainty, where plans might go awry, and small variations in conditions might have made a telling difference. All were, in short, isolated moments where it is possible to ask 'What if?' All hung in the balance, and offer for the viewer of a film treatment the frisson of seeing how the drama played itself out on a human level where the actions of the individual might have some consequence. The grand sweep of historical narrative becomes comprehensible in miniature, and the individual is presented as being able to 'make a difference' in circumstances where the outcome was so uncertain and not already decided by sheer weight of numbers or an imbalance in available *matériel*.

For the player or reader of the game-fiction text such moments of apparent historical indecision, where things might have gone one way or another, allow for the interpolation of the self who moves the mouse and adjusts the variables, a move that seems to restore the importance of individual agency that is so often swamped in the military histories that rely on the representation of an extended narrative sweep, presenting military forces as dehumanised machines. More recent American-led conflicts, particularly the Gulf War that had so exercised Baudrillard, would have made a poor game at a strategic level because of their dependence on a doctrine of overwhelming military force, where the military machine renders the individual inconsequential. There is an absence of any significant doubt with regard to broad outcome. The

'What if?' of this kind of counterfactual enquiry takes a point at which there is no inevitability of outcome, even when narrativised in tellings that depend on establishing causality. It might have been so different – it might have turned out some other way.

Before examining the particularity of the 'realism' of *Close Combat* and its attempt to produce a specific form of verisimilitude in detail, however, we should remind ourselves that it makes no attempt at all at the visual simulation of a first-person point of view, and that it deliberately foregrounds the artificiality of the playing or reading experience. The interpolation of the reader does not attempt to place him or her 'in' the text, but allows him or her to ask questions of the text from a critical distance. The player or reader has the opportunity not to imagine that he or she might 'change history' through individual action, but that he or she might tell something other the received narrative account already told by so many others. In the 'space between' fact and fiction we are given licence to ask 'What if?' This is a game-fiction for armchair generals, and not for those who want access to an ersatz combat experience. It makes no more claim to being able to magically 'transport' the reader into the past than does the work of military history, and less than is claimed for genre war novels. There are first-person games that have eschewed the milieu of genre science fiction and been set firmly within the Second World War (such as *Medal of Honor: Allied Assault*), or used it for its visual reference with a far more relaxed attitude towards verisimilitude, such as *Return to Castle Wolfenstein* (2002), but this is not one of them.[10]

The management screens of *Close Combat* are not just where you find yourself when you 'die' as in *Half-Life*, or even when you wish to consult your inventory, as in *Tomb Raider*, but are an integral part of the game. In *Close Combat: Battle of the Bulge*, for example, the player has access to at least four different levels of management screen in which he or she can both acquire information and adjust variables. A 'Command' screen allows the alteration of 'realism settings' that affect the ways in which the game is played, a 'Battle Group' screen allows the perusal of broad unit details, which are then provided on a soldier-by-soldier basis on the 'Soldier' screen. A 'Strategic Map' allows the monitoring and movement of units on the whole Ardennes front. This might not be an answer to a Gradgrindian demand for 'facts, facts, facts', but it does satisfy any possible desire for 'data, data, data'. A fifth possibility, a 'Scenario Editor' that allows the player to change all the strategic details, allows any player an even more obvious illusion of 'authorship', allowing a change to be made to almost every aspect of the campaign mode of the game.

Given this absolute rejection of the mimetic possibility of immersive gameplay, we are in absolutely no danger of mistaking 'simulation' for 'real' in the encounter with a wargame like *Close Combat*, even if we can imagine this to be a future possibility for a game such as *Half-Life*. That the player adopts the role of a military commander is an obvious conceit. Where the camera of *Half-Life* had allowed a limited pretence that what 'Freeman sees' is what 'I see', the point of view of the in-game camera when playing out the battles of *Close Combat* is one unavailable within experience, and not located within an alternative psychology. There is no equivalent of a Freeman or a Lara Croft, no 'body' in which this point of view is housed. The all-seeing eye of the player floats at a fixed point above events, able to distinguish enough details so that he or she can discriminate between types of units and types of terrain, and so play the game effectively, but the player is always kept at a distance. Like the presence of the omniscient or near-omniscient narrator of literary fiction, this point of view reminds us of the artificiality of the vision we have access to, and acts to distance us from any possibility of mimesis.

The player of *Close Combat* observes from overhead, and is offered a bird's-eye view of a landscape that resembles the miniaturised world of the model railway far more than it does the real world. Although many real-time strategy games have made the most of technological advances unavailable to the early episodes of *Close Combat*, and deploy a three dimensional floating camera that can swoop and climb, (both *Shogun: Total War* (2000) and *Black & White* (2001) have done so to particularly impressive visual effect, for example) the movement of the camera available to the player in *Close Combat* is restricted to the simple possibilities of up and down, left and right. Even when the amount of the screen devoted to the portrayal of an ongoing battle is expanded to its maximum size it is not entirely given over to a view of the battlefield. At the bottom of the screen is an information bar that gives details of whatever unit was last highlighted by the cursor, as well as more general information about the current state of play, and a selection of recent messages from the troops. The cursor remains visible at all times, as it does when we are working within Windows. In the later games in the series, a left click offers important tactical information about each point of terrain (what it is, the amount of cover it offers, the height etc.). Rather than concentrate on pleasing visual effect, the utility of the screen image as a conduit of information is prioritised.

If all the possible pop-up information windows and menus in *Close Combat* are turned on, then the actual playing area becomes remarkably restricted, with a small summary map of the entire battlefield, information on the current activity, state of mind, weapon carried, ammunition remaining, etc, of each and every soldier in the unit currently highlighted. And this information can be almost overwhelmingly detailed – there are sixteen possible 'morale states' for each individual soldier in *Close Combat: Battle of the Bulge*, for example. *Half-Life* had rationalised the presence of on-screen information by asserting that this was part of the HUD (the 'Head-Up Display' that one finds in the helmets of fighter pilots, for example) built into Freeman's HEV ('Hostile Environment') suit. *Close Combat* offers no such rationale for the presence of so much on-screen data. The point of view available, and the concentration on the communication of this wealth of data, contributes to something about this type of game-fiction that needs to be emphasised, that *Close Combat* is a wargame, and that its form of 'realism' acts through the imposition of a vast range of limits on possible action and rules that constrain possibility, rather than on the conferring of the kinds of freedoms of reading that had been so central to the success of *Half-Life* or *Tomb Raider*. This game-fiction, in which important orders are often greeted with messages from the troops that they 'Can't go there' or 'We can't hurt that', is not going to appeal to those who were frustrated by Lara Croft's occasional 'no'.

Even the inclusion of the term 'real-time' in 'real-time strategy' game indicates a limit that constrains. Originally used to denote the difference between this form of text where the game moves on no matter what we do or do not do (in effect reading 'inaction' as an 'action'), and those earlier games which were based on two sides taking their turns independently, it has a slightly different effect in a game-fiction such as *Close Combat* than it has in a game less concerned with verisimilitude such as *Command & Conquer*. In most real-time strategy games the abolition of the turn-based system of the board game was a method of taking advantage of the technology of the computer to speed things up to match the expectations of a general contemporary audience not always prepared to suffer the plodding arrangement of units and orders that had characterised the more complex traditional boardgames. The old saw about warfare being comprised of long periods of inactivity followed by short periods of intense excitement would certainly apply to the experience of playing a Second World War boardgame such as 'Squad Leader', for example. The juggling of *Command & Conquer* units in 'real-time' is far more frenetic, and comparable to the circus performer keeping the plates spinning on their poles. In *Close Combat*, however, 'real-time' means that heavy armour cannot move at high speed, tired units or heavily equipped engineers limp about the battlefield, and generally slows down the game. On the one hand this is a gesture towards the form of realism that *Close Combat* establishes through comparison (it does not have the obviously absurd command system of *Command & Conquer* where units sprint from place to place with a cheerful response of 'Yessir'), and on the other it makes another claim for seriousness of intent. Demand instant gratification and you will be very disappointed as your heavy tank trundles forward with glacial slowness.

As the continuing popularity of chess indicates, the basic and restrictive 'rules' of war have long been recognised as providing a convenient rationale and structure that can be borrowed for a diverting game between two individuals. There is no need for a complex narrative justification for the game – two 'armies' meet on the battlefield and the aim of each player is to force the other to capitulate. All the possible moves are known to both players. There is no element of chance in this game, no rolling of dice, no betting of everything on the turn of the next card. The meaning produced through the playing of the game speaks not about one's understanding of military history or tactics, but about the comparative 'intellect' of the players. Players of chess have achieved an intellectual respectability that players of other wargames must regard with envy. Chess is surrounded with an aura of sophistication, and in its abstract complexity seems to belong, like the literature of high modernism or the installations of contemporary art, to an intellectual elite – or at least to a bourgeoisie who would like to believe they belong within that elite. Moving a carefully painted 1/72nd scale Airfix model of a Sherman tank across terrain made from polystyrene ceiling tiles while holding a tape measure in your other hand has never quite been seen in the same way.

And yet chess, as much as *Close Combat*, remains a stylised representation of war. As a signifier of intellectual superiority it even found itself functioning as a substitute for actual warfare when Fischer and Spassky fought their Cold War battles in Reykjavik in 1972. However abstract the pieces, even if one is playing with a novelty set with characters taken from *Alice in Wonderland*, chess remains a wargame, its poor bloody infantry being the pawns, its elite troops the rooks, bishops and queens, and its mobile cavalry in the form of the knights. This might never have been a very 'realistic' approximation of warfare as experienced on the front line, but it does reproduce the abstraction to which battles are often reduced in some forms of military history. The military historian might represent the progress of battles with little boxes and arrows on maps that do not reduce the specific geography that was fought over to the flat abstraction of an eight by eight chessboard, but he or she is similarly dealing with the stylised rather than the real, with conventions of representation that are analogous to a set of 'rules'.

Close Combat is not chess, being both more complex and straightforward as a game, with its myriad of statistics and variables working away behind the scenes, and in its reliance on the vagaries of chance, but it is similarly an abstraction of the experience of war that might portray and even name the individual soldiers seen moving across the screen, but does not so much refer directly to the 'real' but to the way that the real has been represented both within other games and within historical narratives. Its purpose, however, is not so much to produce a 'winner' or signal the intellectual superiority of human over machine, but to tell (and retell) a story. As a game-fiction it remains a primarily visual form of representation, despite the mass of words that appear on the screen and its demand for conventional literacy. As such it adapts the move available to the historian who would evade the potential complications of 'telling' (obviously 'subjective', with the historian controlling narrative) and appear to be 'showing' (apparently 'objective', with the historian apparently absent) what happens. This is not a move towards mimesis in this context, but towards the Rankean fiction of historical revelation of an existing narrative already embedded in the historical field. *Close Combat*'s integration of visual archive material and maps to make its claims for authenticity are nothing new, of course, and would even have been familiar to Harold Krebs, the traumatised First World War veteran of Ernest Hemingway's short story 'Soldier's Home' (1925):

> He sat there on the porch reading a book on the war. It was a
> history and he was reading about all the engagements he had
> been in. It was the most interesting reading he had ever done.
> He wished there were more maps. He looked forward with a
> good feeling to reading all the really good histories when they
> came out with good detail maps. Now he was really learning
> about the war.[11]

And it is significant that while waiting for the publication of such
'really good histories' through which he might make sense of his
personal experiences, Krebs takes refuge in the sports pages of his
local newspaper. As a veteran who has experienced a collapse in his
faith in 'consequences' Krebs's need to look to games and the history books that are to come for his structures of meaning is understandably extreme. But it nevertheless dramatises the way in which
both games (where events make clear sense according to agreed
frameworks of rules) and histories that in their 'good detail[ed]
maps' would prioritise 'showing' over 'telling', answer a basic human need. This abstraction of war as game with its own plethora
of detailed maps in *Close Combat* similarly provides a way of engaging with the historical record in the search for some provisional
and contingent historical narrative that might restore or confirm
our own faith in causality and allow the individual some place,
however problematic, within the narratives of history. The desire
for such abstraction might not be particularly laudable, and telling
war stories, whether by the propagandist, the bar-room raconteur,
or the historian might erase the horror of the event in a way that
might disturb us, as Krebs observes in 'Soldier's Home'. It answers
the basic human impulse to create historical narratives, and to put
our faith in those interpretative narratives where history pretends
to just present us with 'facts' rather than risk narrativisation and
the accompanying implications of 'fictionality'.

If apparent sense might be made of the past through a reliance on the formalisation of mapping and the structure of games,
then, it should not surprise us that games that make historical

reference resemble historical moves to make sense of the past. In terms of other wargames, *Close Combat* owes most to those table-top wargames played with little lumps of lead cast to represent infantry and tanks and moved over a table top. Unless the player has an inordinately large monitor the scale at which *Close Combat* is usually played even reproduces the approximate scale of $1/300^{th}$ 'microtanks' that is a standard in table-top wargaming. Chess has relatively few rules, while *Close Combat*, like the heavy rulebooks for such wargames, has many – but the rules of *Close Combat* are invisible and do not have to be learned in the same way as those of chess, or consulted at every stage of play as in table-top games. Instead they operate through an appeal to 'common sense' that is central to what the producers mean by 'realism'. As the manual for one episode explains:

> *Close Combat: Invasion Normandy* is a real-time strategy game that puts the emphasis on REAL. During a battle, you command up to 15 units ranging from squads of infantry to heavy tanks. The soldiers under your command act like real soldiers. If you order them to exert themselves, they get tired, if the enemy shoots at them, they keep their heads down, and when in danger they get scared. If a soldier becomes too scared, he may stop listening to orders; he may even surrender or desert.

There is something intriguing about this understanding of realism that also relates to the claims that had been made for the 'sophistication' of the artificial intelligence of *Half-Life*'s opponents. The artificial intelligence of *Close Combat*, like that of *Half-Life*, moves opposing units and issues orders as if there was a human opponent facing the player or imprisoned within the body of the machine. The comparative sophistication of the artificial intelligence in such circumstances is expressed in how closely the game-fiction offers a convincing analogue of a human opponent, while still allowing the narrative to progress.[12] But in *Close Combat* it also affects the in-game behaviour of the units supposedly under the control of the player. The test here is against whether what is attempted 'makes sense' according to what is known about small unit tactics and the behaviour of human beings in combat. In *Command & Conquer* it was often possible to win a game by throwing as many units as possible forward in a mad rush. Such attempts to replay the death or glory of the charge of the Light Brigade in *Close Combat* are not only likely to result in the same kind of defeat that occurred in the Crimea, but to be impossible.

The artificial intelligence of *Close Combat* provides its troops with something that expresses itself in behaviour that pretends to their possession of a sense of self-preservation. In order to take a heavily defended building the player would be best advised to lay down covering fire, use available terrain sensibly or lay down smoke barrages, and only charge forwards when enemy resistance is likely to have been minimised. We do not, however, have to think of such actions in the language of the 'rules' of the game – the mortar barrage will go on for four 'turns'; wait until the 'morale state' of the enemy drops from 'healthy' to 'pinned' etc. – but in the language already available to describe lived experience. Our troops are 'scared' or 'berserk', and the player can tell that by their actions without consulting the rules or the pop-up menus, they are not expressed as numerical modifications to the various equations that underpin the workings of the game.

The usual description of such an interface would refer to it as 'intuitive', but this is not really adequate. There are mystical assumptions about 'intuition' that would be out of place in reference to game-fictions. One does not need intuition to know that if one steps out into the road in the path of oncoming traffic one is likely to be run over. This is far more a matter of acting on the basis of prior observation of the world. Similarly 'common sense' dictates that the player does not order his or her troops to charge a machine-gun nest over open ground.

Counterfactual gameplay

In a sense, *Close Combat* shows a clear recognition that the counterfactual text essentially 'earns' its right to deviate from received historical narratives by establishing the credentials from which it starts. In its campaign mode it allows the player to watch the incremental increase of deviation depending on apparently minor variations on the details of the historical record. This might be thought of as the 'snowball effect' of much speculative fiction. Deviation from the observed world (what some science fiction critics would call the 'novum' that separates science fiction from other fiction) might be relatively minor – an important road junction held a little longer here, a bridge blown there – but its consequences as they are played out might lead to the construction of a very different narrative from that of the received historical account.[13] The snowball tossed away at the top of the mountain might appear insignificant at that moment, but the inhabitants of the village below might have good reason to fear the avalanche.

This calls to mind the Ray Bradbury story 'A Sound of Thunder' (most often read as concerned, supposedly, with temporal paradox rather than with the mutability of the historical text) where the careless destruction of a single butterfly by a group of time-trippers off exploring in the past plunges their 'present' into fascist tyranny.[14] *Close Combat* does not allow its own snowballs to grow so big, but it is possible to construct 'endings' that in their obvious fictionality represent a considerable shift from the 'facts'. Arnhem can be taken with all the bridges intact, and Allied armour can prepare to drive into the heart of Germany. The Normandy landings can be stopped in their tracks, and the Americans (and there are only American units included here, just as there were in *Saving Private Ryan*) thrown back into the sea. The German armies can drive through the Ardennes and set off in a race towards Antwerp, potentially altering not just the course, but the outcome, of the Second World War. Only in *Close Combat III: The Russian Front*, can the player not change the story of the historical event in a major way, with the final battle taking place at the fall of Berlin no matter how 'well' or effectively one plays out the individual fragments of the narrative.

Even this episode of *Close Combat* shows recognition that it is the creation of an extended narrative, rather than the playing out of the individual events, that is central to *Close Combat*, as the manual for *Close Combat III* makes clear:

> Your men in the trenches respond like real soldiers – they react authentically to the stress of combat and are affected by their fatigue level, ability, physical and mental condition, and other factors. The game adds a role-playing element by making you the commander of a fire brigade – a special company of elite troops moving among hot spots on the Eastern Front. You are responsible for keeping your men alive and for advancing your own rank, which, in turn, increases the size and quality of your forces. As the four years of conflict pass and both German and Russian technology improves, you can add new and better weapons to your arsenal.

The counterfactual fiction might change some of the 'facts', but it never disposes of the need for causal narrative linkage between those facts. It might tell a different story, but it remains diachronic (sequential in time), progressive in its assumptions (moving from a beginning to an ending) and dependent on our understanding of cause and effect. What we do 'now' has 'later' effect. Time equates with improvement. This operates on the level of the individual component of our forces (we are responsible for keeping our men 'alive' to fight another day) as well as at the level of the campaigns of those episodes when we are invited to see the extent of the damage our counterfactual snowball can do.

All of this potential for multiple outcomes requires extensive computing power. What computers have always been good at, fortunately, is the storage of such vast amounts of empirical data. Unfortunately, software designers have not always been quite so good at providing a user-friendly interface, a 'front-end', that allows the recovery and manipulation of that data in a manner that meets the needs of the individual user. What a game-fiction like *Close Combat* seems to show the first glimmerings of is a text–user interface that allows access to a mass of data (the details of weapons performance, unit deployments, weather conditions, equations that model behaviour under set environmental conditions etc.) and operates through the application of apparent 'common sense' in that we do not have to remember the abstract 'rule' that will be applicable in a particular instant, but work with our knowledge of the observed world.

In a very small way the text then allows the construction of a counterfactual fiction, particularly when the readings of the individual textual fragments, the battles, are linked to form an extended narrative in the campaign mode. We approach the mass of empirical data not as the historian who would seek answers to basic causal questions of why one event follows another, but as the writer or reader of the counterfactual fictions who begs the question of what might have happened 'if' such and such a variable is changed. As it stands, such questions as can be asked of a game-fiction such as *Close Combat* are extremely limited in form (although they include some of the classic speculative enquiries of military historians, such as 'What if the German armoured units had been positioned right behind the beach defences in Normandy?' or 'What if the Americans had air support constantly available throughout the Ardennes offensive?') But this kind of text does not just allow such forms of enquiry, as conventional historical narratives do. Rather, it depends upon its audience having a desire to do so.

It might be worth spending some time considering the distinction between the historical work and the work of fiction that Hayden White had offered up in *Metahistory*:

> Unlike literary fictions, such as the novel, historical works are made up of events that exist outside the consciousness of the writer. The events reported in a novel can be invented in a way that they cannot be (or are not supposed to be) in a history. This makes it difficult to distinguish between the chronicle of events and the story being told in a literary fiction ... Unlike

the novelist the historian confronts a veritable chaos of events *already constituted*, out of which he must choose the elements of the story he would tell. He makes his story by including some events and excluding others, by stressing some and subordinating others. This process of exclusion, stress, and subordination is carried out in the interest of constituting *a story of a particular kind*. That is, he 'emplots' his story.[15]

The reader of *Close Combat* might not function as the historian is understood, here, to function, but nor does he or she function as the writer of the literary fiction. The 'archive' or historical field in which she or she works is already subject to the choices of inclusion and exclusion that White notes, the basic emplotment is already extant in the selection of the individual moments of intervention that have been selected for us by the games designers (there is no prospect, for example, of outflanking the maps on offer, or of pulling in troops from other fronts). But it is in the possibility of intervening in the processes of stress and subordination, of being able to tinker with the footnotes and details of this emplotted narrative, as well as being able to construct a divergent narrative, that means that *Close Combat* stands out from other forms of historical storytelling. We might have to tell 'a story of a particular kind' (a progressive and diachronic military history), but we can tell it in a way that puts the responsibility for the 'process' of construction, as much as responsibility for the advance of our forces, in the person of the reader.

Close Combat does not just allow its players to compare the narrative they construct through the progression of the campaign game against the historical record, it insists that they do so. In *Close Combat II: A Bridge Too Far* this had taken the form of video clips of archive footage that can be played out telling not the story of the operation constructed through the playing of the game, but a documentary account of the received historical version of events. It is quite possible to be firmly in control of the bridge at Arnhem while watching an account of the surrender of those very forces on screen. In *Close Combat IV: The Battle of the Bulge* or *Close Combat: Invasion Normandy* the progress made within the game is always compared on the information screen that follows an individual engagement with historical event, and the player is told whether they are progressing 'better' or 'worse' than their historical counterparts. One is not in a contest against the computer's artificial intelligence, but with a historical narrative. This double move of deviation and reference is a characteristic feature of much counterfactual fiction. Unlike that speculative or extrapolative science fiction that it resembles in its imagination of possibility (although orientated not towards the future but the past) this form of game-fiction remains anxious to remind us that the deviation from the record and the events already constituted are not too extreme, and that this is an essentially historical enterprise that is not simply 'untrue' (like the fictionalisation of the capture of a German Enigma machine by American naval forces in the film *U–571* (2000) that was greeted with outrage in the UK as an example of the falsification of history that demanded an on-screen disclaimer to 'set the record straight') but brings us back to consideration of that record.

Philip K. Dick's *The Man in the High Castle* had imagined a world in which the Axis powers had won the Second World War and partitioned the United States, but it offered up an alternative narrative through the casting of the yarrow stalks of the I-Ching and the 'novel' *The Grasshopper Lies Heavy*, that reminded the reader that this was not a text that could be read without reference to received historical narratives. When Robert Harris also constructed his alternative world in which the Third Reich had won the war in *Fatherland*, his text focused on the danger of practices of 'fiction making' through the subordination of the historical event in its concentration on its protagonist's retrieval of evidence of the Final Solution. *Close Combat* might not have such textual ambition, or approach the sophistication of telling of either text, but it comes from the same place, departing from the received historical account in order to focus the reader's attention back upon it. *Close Combat* then remains a text to be read alongside the conventional historical work, and not in some way to supplant it.

Notes

1 A more obvious choice of representative Second World War wargame might have been *Sudden Strike* (2000), which has managed to reach a non-specialist non-wargaming general audience in a way that *Close Combat* has not. Although it is also a real-time strategy game viewed from an isometric top-down perspective, and similarly pays lavish attention to period detail, at least in terms of the visual representation of individual units, *Sudden Strike* does not display the level of narrative possibility that is the focus of this chapter.

2 Cited in Linda Hutcheon, *A Poetics of Postmodernism: History, Theory, Fiction* (London: Routledge, 1988), p. 113. De Man's thinking about matters of rhetoric and narrative informs much of his volume of essays *Blindness and Insight: Essays in the Rhetoric of Contemporary Criticism* (London: Routledge, 1983), but his essay on Georg Lukács might be of most interest to critics interested in this aspect of game-fictions, pp. 51–9.

3 I owe my understanding of how the historical work is written to Hayden White's account in *Metahistory: The Historical Imagination in Nineteenth-Century Europe* (Baltimore, MD: Johns Hopkins University Press), that takes narrative theory (through Northrop Frye's *Anatomy of Criticism: Four Essays* (Princeton, NJ: Princeton University Press, 1957)) to historiography. See White's introduction TO *Metahistory*, pp. 1–43. White's work also represents an important development in the increasing recognition in the late twentieth century that as written text historical narrative required examination for what White terms the 'ideological implication' of the emplotments that it 'constructs' rather than somehow 'discovers' already extant in the historical field. White's *Tropics of Discourse: Essays in Cultural Criticism* (London: Johns Hopkins University Press, 1978) and Dominic LaCapra's *Rethinking Intellectual History: Texts, Contexts, Language* (Ithaca, NY: Cornell University Press, 1983) will also be useful to anyone seeking to trace the beginnings of the internal debates that have taken place within academic historiography.

4 For a conventional account of the impact that Ranke's mantra has had on academic historiography since the 1830s, see E. H. Carr, *What is History* (Harmondsworth: Penguin, 1964), pp. 8–9. A less convinced account is on offer in Arthur Marwick, *The Nature of History* (London: Macmillan, 1970), pp. 36–8.

5 Jean Baudrillard, *The Gulf War Did Not Take Place*, trans. Paul Patton (Bloomington and Indianapolis, IN: Indiana University Press, 1995), p. 43.

6 The extent to which *Medal of Honor* makes deliberate allusions to this film might be apparent in the joke that did the rounds of Internet discussion groups shortly after a video of the Normandy sequence was released, referring to *Medal of Honor* as 'Quick-Saving Private Ryan'.

7 See Steven Poole, *Trigger Happy: the Inner Life of Videogames* (London: Fourth Estate, 2000), pp. 48–9.

8 I would hesitate to make any necessary association between *Close Combat*'s serious engagement with history and assumptions about the 'maturity', chronological or otherwise, of its readership. It is worth noting, however, that this is a form of game-fiction – the wargame – that has been largely confined to development for the PC, rather than on the various consoles that are the dominant mode of playing by younger players. *Tomb Raider* is a game that has always been available in both game consoles and PC formats, and *Half-Life* finally made the transition from PC to console in 2001. Like *SimCity*, or a spreadsheet-based game such as *Championship Manager*, *Close Combat* makes the most not of the graphics capabilities of the PC, but of its ability to crunch numbers.

9 What is meant by 'historical fiction' has long been subject to critical debate (see Hutcheon, *Poetics of Postmodernism*, pp. 113–15 for a brief account of some contributions in relation to the historical novel), but I use the term here in relation to game-fictions in the sense that there is a conscious foregrounding of historical verisimilitude within the contract of reading of the self-declared historical fiction.

10 And there is something troubling in the way that some fictions, and particularly *Wolfenstein 3D* (1992) (the first recognisable first-person shooter that attempted an illusion of potential immersion) and its sequel *Return to Castle Wolfenstein*, use reference to the Second World

War as another strategy to protect themselves from possible critique of their violent content. It is OK to 'kill' the on-screen enemies in both games because they are not 'human'. But rather than move to the presentation of the obviously dehumanised aliens of a game such as *Half-Life*, both *Wolfenstein* titles dress their enemies in Nazi uniforms. Such a move made with reference to the Third Reich would seem to be far more problematic than at first might appear, and somewhat tasteless in even such an obviously fictional text.

11 Ernest Hemingway, *In Our Time* (New York: Scribner, 1958), p. 72.

12 It should be noted that the artificial intelligence in most strategy games available in the late 1990s and early years of the twenty-first century is disappointing in this respect, with units making inexplicable moves, and failing to respond to the player with any particular evidence of forward planning. Chess computers might have been able to take on Grand Masters with some degree of success, but the AI of game-fictions rarely threatens to reproduce the human. There is no hunch-back in the machine, as was allegorised by Walter Benjamin as 'historical materialism' in his 'Theses on the Philosophy of History' (see Benjamin, *Illuminations: Essays and Reflections*, trans. Harry Zohn (London: Cape, 1970), pp. 245–55, p. 245), and the interesting shift in expectation is that we are disappointed to find that there is no hunch-back in the machine. It is the recognition that the beige box contains something less than a human player that generates regret – not the discovery of deception, but its absence.

13 See Adam Roberts, *Science Fiction* (London: Routledge, 2000), pp. 17–27. For a fuller understanding of the term 'novum' see Darko Suvin, *Metamorphoses of Science Fiction: On the Poetics and History of a Literary Genre* (London and New Haven, CT: Yale University Press, 1979).

14 This story, which is frequently anthologised, was originally published in Ray Bradbury, *The Golden Apples of the Sun and Other Stories*, New York: Hart Davis, 1953.

15 Hayden White, *Metahistory*, p. 6. Emphasis in original.

Managing the real: reading *SimCity*

SimCity [inc. *SimCity* (1989), *SimCity 2000* (1993), *SimCity 3000* (1999)] Management simulation. The game is played on a map grid containing randomly assigned geographical and topological features (hills, rivers, lakes, forests). The player oversees the development of a city within this landscape through control of a budget that allows the zoning of land areas for particular usage (residential, commercial, industrial) and the placement of urban infrastructure (power, education, transport etc.). Each calendar year in which the player sets budget controls represents one standard 'turn', but the player is allowed to intervene in such matters at any time. There is some attempt to reflect the development of technology over time with various possibilities only unlocked at certain historical points (nuclear power or airports, for example). Natural disasters may occur randomly or be instigated by the player. There is no clear end to the game or absolute objective to be achieved.

The focus on *SimCity* as the final extended example in this study may come as something of a relief for those readers who find the concentration on the representation of violence within the computer game to be either worrying or simply tiresome. *SimCity* does not allow its player to wage war on other cities except in the vaguest of economic terms, opportunities for death or glory are few and far between, and even the request that the military might be allowed to set up a base within the city can be rejected by the more pacifistic player. There is no 'fire' button hidden among the controls or keyboard shortcuts of *SimCity*. Perhaps for this very reason its inclusion alongside narrative game-fictions driven forwards by their move from moment to moment of extreme violence might

also come as something of a surprise. Forms of conflict and con-
frontation have always played a major part in the structuring of
both games and popular fictions, after all. We know where we are,
in story terms, where there is a loaded gun available and a slavering
alien or shambling zombie in front of us. How we 'should', or how
we 'can', read such a plot fragment is obvious.

Where *Tomb Raider* and *Half-Life* had obvious narrative
pretensions in their reliance on the telling of lengthy 'quest' or 'escape' narratives with a strong drive towards the specific conclusion
of an already emplotted story, and *Close Combat*'s campaigns
showed its potential for the construction of an extended
counterfactual narrative, any comparable narrative ambition in
SimCity is less than obvious. As the manual for *SimCity 2000* informs the new player, this is a different kind of text: 'When you play
SimCity 2000, you become the planner, designer and mayor of an
unlimited number of cities. You can take over and run any of the
included scenario cities, or build your own from the ground up.'

Even the use of the word 'unlimited' would seem to declare this to be anything but a means of constructing a clearly identifiable narrative. What we are being invited to construct is a model
of a city, and not a story. In *SimCity* you adopt the role of a mayor
who controls a city from the moment of its foundation, involved
in the manipulation of far more financial and physical variables
than were available, even, to the player of *Close Combat*. Variations
would appear to be near-infinite in the extent of their possible combinations. This text is so '*scriptable*', to use Roland Barthes' term,
that it may appear as almost unreadable as text. 'You' watch 'your'
city grow and change over time, zooming in and out of the screen
to observe the daily lives of 'your' citizens in as much detail as 'you'
want. 'You' can even switch off the menu bars and watch 'your' city
ticking over without being reminded that 'you' can intervene. There
are no fights to win, no exploration to undertake, no puzzles to
solve. *SimCity 3000* even disposes of those optional 'scenarios' of
SimCity 2000 that had demanded that the player deal with the after-

effects of recession, terrorism, flood, fire, or act of little green men in flying saucers. In *SimCity 3000* there might be pre-designed maps featuring already established settlements, but there is no obvious equivalent to the missions or battles of more aggressive games, or the scenarios of its precursors in the series. If there is a form of narrative identifiable within *SimCity*, and the argument throughout this chapter is that there is, then it does not write itself in big letters across the landscape, explain itself in the manuals, or make itself clear in the simplistic equation of gun-plus-zombies-equals-press-fire-button. Instead of negotiation within any recognisable plot, this kind of text concentrates on apparently handing over the responsibility of authorship to 'you' to such an extent that it no longer resembles traditional narrative at all. 'You' (the reader) are present, but there is an absence of any author. We have a 'beginning', and a 'middle', but to borrow Frank Kermode's phrase, we have no 'sense of an ending'.[1]

It is the intensity of this apparent liberation from any form of clearly emplotted narrative, its foregrounding of the 'open-ended' rather than 'closed' experience on offer that was only hinted at in the other game-fictions discussed so far, that is so fascinating in *SimCity*. In some ways *SimCity* is far more exemplary of this alternative open-ended method of engaging with computer-based texts than the other specific titles I focus on, and resembles traditional narrative forms the least. How this can be thought through as a form of narrative telling rarely possible outside of the game-fiction, rather than something other than narrative, and other than a somehow realist narrative, will be the focus of this chapter. In eradicating the singular ending that conditions so many of the meanings we acquire from our other forms of text, *SimCity* appears to be breaking a fundamental rule of narrative but remains, perhaps paradoxically, a readable text as well as a playable game. As such this chapter looks at this game-fiction as more than just an example of a specific genre or type of game (the management or 'god game'), but as representative of a basic difference between how story might be told and read within computer games and how our other stories are read and told.

Both *Half-Life* and *Tomb Raider* have had their direct clones, but few have been able to compete with them directly in story terms, even when more advanced technology has been made available to designers who then ratchet up our visual and aural expectations. We recognise their stories because they resemble the stories we are exposed to in our other forms of popular fiction, and when we make aesthetic judgements we compare them both with those other stories, as well as with the stories offered in other computer games. As such they were chosen as particularly appropriate examples of their genres for the purposes of this study because they are texts where the narrative possibilities of game-fiction as a form were comparatively effectively realised. With *SimCity* we have relatively direct clones that offer minimal variation on the basic theme of city building and take it to the management of railway systems, theme parks, and space stations, among other social and business structures. But not only do we do see dozens of 'sim' games that can be seen to belong firmly in the genre that *SimCity* is representative of, but we see many more games within other genres take on board its central claim for free-form potential and 'unlimited' possibility. As with *Close Combat*, this is a narrative of enquiry based on the premise of the 'What if?' that operates through engagement with the world of the game 'as if' observation of the world can reliably inform our choices of intervention.

And yet by operating in this 'sim' universe with only a comparatively loose connection with the observed world, it is open to far more extreme departures from that world than had been possible in *Close Combat*. It is the apparent lack of constraint in disposing of any limits on the possibility of outcome that this chapter explores, and this implication that we have access, here, not to single texts but to a near infinite number of texts, that is interrogated. That popular fiction is essentially formulaic is a common enough negative observation – and *SimCity* is almost nothing but a collection of formulae given graphical expression on screen. Even so, this kind of formula fiction is full of contradictions: formulaic, but unpredictable; open-ended, but always nudged in particular directions; visually unrealistic, but grounded in our understanding of the observed world; 'sim', but not 'simulation'.

The producers of *SimCity* hit paydirt early with their adaptation of one of the more prosaic uses of computers, the modelling of complex systems for economic or scientific purposes, for the basic structure of a game. *SimCity* is, in computer game terms, an old and venerable games franchise that has barely changed in its basic gameplay that relies on such computer modelling since its first release.[2] Despite a series of creeping improvements in the graphics over the lifetime of the series, it remains closer to those abstract models that are toyed with by academic and business economists than to what we generally think of as text. As an exceptionally (and perhaps surprisingly) successful series it established the basic mechanics of resource management that do not just appear in other 'sim' games, but are now often integrated as a part of many other games that then add a strong story element to it.[3] As the exploration of an exemplary text this consideration of *SimCity* is offered as a way of looking in detail at some of the claims made for game-fictions regarding their apparent freedom of possible outcome when they seem to depart radically from the linearity of the emplotted narrative. As a product of mass consumer culture, in a world where our politicians throw the word 'choice' around with abandon and our other forms of text emphasise a lack of closure and celebrate narrative uncertainty, *SimCity* appears to offer access to a plurality of choice and individual experience within the mass product of consumer capitalism. As the use of the term 'god-game' to describe such game-fictions implies, there is something about such management games that can be seen as empowering and liberating – we are not the passive consumer of this product of mass popular culture, we are allowed the illusion of not only 'human' but 'godly' agency.

The fact that we are playing a computer game, and that our 'godly' powers are incredibly circumscribed by the rules of its operation should not be forgotten, however. The fantasy of control it offers might even point up the powerlessness most of us experience in the world. As with *Close Combat*, we are not invited to 'immerse' ourselves in this text. Graphically, *SimCity* makes no attempt at any kind of visual realism. It has rather basic but jolly graphics that are colourfully exemplary of types rather than straightforwardly realistic, resembling the restricted but vibrant palette of the worlds of children's television rather than the contemporary city that we live in. In what sense, then, might it be meaningful to include *SimCity* among the other 'realist' game-fictions of this study that focuses so much on questions of narrative? In terms of realism, it might make the same kind of claim for accuracy of representation in its mathematical modeling that the economist might make of his or her computer model (of the balance between distance travelled and the attractiveness of a particular location for habitation, or the effect of high crime rates on property values, for example), but it does not seem to relate to the real in a clear way, and certainly not in a manner comparable to a game-fiction such as *Close Combat*. This is graphically and ideologically a game based firmly in the United States, whatever international landmarks are placed in the middle of the map, but it does not describe itself as such. What we have here is a 'sim city' located within a 'sim nation' populated by individual 'sims' who spend 'simoleons'. 'Sim' as a contraction or truncation of 'simulation' makes clear what the title of *Half-Life* had only hinted at – this kind of 'simulation' is not an attempt to elide distance between text and world, but is situated always at a distance, and in that distance 'between' rests its fictional possibility.

It also displays little of the visual sobriety already ascribed to *Close Combat*. In a sense this is a game-fiction that is inherently 'realistic' in the most basic of its workings, always insisting on the causal relationship between actions and never allowing the impossible leap or the infinite ammunition of Lara Croft's pistols in *Tomb*

Raider. The game's designers have not had to make this increasingly *more* realistic in its visual representation as processor power has advanced in leaps and bounds and graphics cards have shouldered some of the burden of computation, but *less* so than the technology allows, in order to signal the most fundamental point that this is a game that provides entertainment and diversion over unproblematic simulation. Where *Close Combat* had attempted to communicate its seriousness ('this is only a game, but it also has historical ambition') *SimCity* attempts to communicate its frivolity ('this is a serious management simulation based on the complex modelling of economic systems, but it is also only a game'). And the games designers have turned to humour as well as its graphical style to communicate that this is supposed to be fun. As with *Half-Life*, where the presence of humour as a strategy intended to disarm some forms of negative critique has already been alluded to in Chapter 3, specific examples of *SimCity*'s playfulness are hard to isolate for the purposes of a work such as this. Whether one finds the constant references to llamas in *SimCity* amusing or not, whether or not we find it funny that the number of pigeons perched on the civic statues of *SimCity* act as an index of our 'success', whether the potted biographies of the advisors we can consult raise a smile or not, and whether the 'sonic yapping-dog' aliens and the excuses for inaction made by the cowering scientists of *Half-Life are* amusing or not is as much a matter of individual reception as to whether one finds a particular comedian funny or offensive, brilliantly original or startlingly crass. What should be noted formally, however, is that all such strategies are obviously intended to amuse, that they communicate that this is not 'just' intended to be an accurate model of the real but that it is also a popular entertainment. This does not mean, however, that *SimCity* is unable to shed light on how the narratives through which we now explain the world to ourselves are beginning to change in their encounter with the computer and the computer game.

The many worlds of *SimCity*

To begin with a discussion of constraints rather than of freedoms, we should recognise that the player has very little direct control over the minutiae of events as they unfold on screen in *SimCity*, as they would in a combat-orientated real-time strategy game. The management of resources is not secondary to some sort of fast-paced action that happens elsewhere, but is the core activity of the game itself. There is no 'battle screen' to go to in *SimCity*, only the grid of the cityscape surrounded by menus and icons. Only when there has been some form of disastrous event that requires inter-vention by the emergency services does the player order individual resources into action. Even then, the speed of *SimCity 3000* runs much slower during a disaster than it does during the game proper. Unlike in *Close Combat*, or any other real-time strategy game, where much attention is given to the possible orders that might be given to each specific unit, and the ability to react quickly to events that haven't been foreseen on a unit-by-unit basis is essential to gameplay, *SimCity* only allows the player to place the police and fire units in proximity to event and let them get on with the job. We are deliberately distanced from the world of the game even more than we were in *Close Combat*. There is no attempt at the construc-tion of any illusion of immersion.

In another notable difference from many game-fictions, the city that is painstakingly crafted and nurtured in *SimCity* has no other function than to be itself. In *Command & Conquer*, *Sid Meier's Civilization II* (1996), *Sid Meier's Alpha Centauri* (1999), *The Settlers III* (1998) or *Age of Empires* (1997), all of which have elements of management built into their structure, there is a need to build something resembling a city or a state, but its function is purely to provide units and/or advance the combat potential of those units. In *Command & Conquer* all buildings, in some way or another, contribute to the war effort. One might research 'Wonders of the World' in *Civilisation II*, build non-combat related buildings in your attempt to reach 'Transcendence' rather than achieve a military victory in *Alpha Centauri*, or build temples in *Age of Empires*, but they all contribute to military output, or at least to defeating an opponent, rather than to the creation of the game-fiction city as an internally satisfying analogue of a functioning city. The temples of *Age of Empires* produce militant priests who are a useful addition to one's military might – they do not minister to the poor or spend their time in good works. Even in a game with a deliberately laid-back and relaxed attitude to building construction where the detailed graphics themselves would not allow for any urgent army building, such as the various instalments of the *Settlers* series, the player still has to take his or her rather mellow military forces against the computer-controlled opponents at some point to win the game.[4] There is nowhere else to spend the accumulated excess capital of a *SimCity* city, no hover-tank upgrades or blazing arrows 'research' to be undertaken, no battle screen to move to where the excess accumulated can be spent as the player advances up the 'tech-tree', no final march upon the enemy that is the ultimate conclusion of the game.[5]

Instead one must balance the budget, invest wisely in infrastructure that degrades over time, and pay close attention to the demands of the citizens. The player can pass city ordinances and change tax rates, build roads and lay down railway tracks, allocate sites for garbage landfill and build schools. A 'news ticker' (a line of text with important 'headlines' detailed) informs the player of the citizens' desires, and petitioners ask for changes in policy. As players of another god game, *Black & White*, found out, such a need to pay attention to competing voices can be as frustrating an experience as keeping a live pet, as travelling 'god-like' over small communities in that game exposes the player to cries that 'we need wood' or 'food, food'. This aspect of management games, often referred to as 'micro-management' and rarely regarded in a positive light by those who hanker after the uncomplicated pleasures of combat, does not appeal to all players, comparable as it is to having to spend your leisure time cleaning out the hamster cage only to be ignored for all your time and effort by a creature that does not understand that we consider ourselves to be engaged in a contractual relationship. Where's the plot? Where's the suspense? Where's the drama? Time passes, but nothing much happens. The closest analogy that springs to mind is the keeping of an ant farm, and, like the 1990s fad for looking after 'Tamagotchis' or playing with on-screen *Petz*, this can appear to be a rather absurd and pointless pastime that bears very little relationship to 'reading', 'solving', or even 'beating' the emplotted narratives of other kinds of game-fiction. The keeping of an ant-farm is hardly storytelling – we might tell stories about our ant farm, but we are unlikely to hold even the most polite audience for too long. This is exaggerated slightly for effect, but from this kind of description it should be apparent that to many players of more immediately satisfying games and game-fictions it can sound as if *SimCity* is hardly recognisable as a game at all, let alone something that might carry a recognisable narrative comparable to that of *Half-Life*, *Tomb Raider*, or even *Close Combat*.

But to substantiate the claim that *SimCity* offers a form of narrative specific to game-fictions, we must look for our comparisons elsewhere. An interesting parallel might perhaps be found in an unlikely source – not in the academic studies of the city or fragments of poetry and prose that the designers at Maxis have drawn upon and sometimes include as appendices in their manuals, but in popular fiction. The opening sections of Terry Pratchett's 'Discworld' series of novels, increasingly concerned itself with the unfolding of his own imaginary city of Ankh-Morpork and the emergence of artificial intelligence in the computer 'Hex', frequently turn to the consideration of matters of narrative form as well as the political, economic and social structures of the city. Pratchett consistently shows an awareness of the processes of textual construction that are implicit in the act of authorship, and sometimes touches on matters of contemporary theorising about how we explain the world to ourselves that even goes beyond narratological theory in its reference. The opening of the novel *Men at Arms*, for example, makes reference to a model for understanding reality borrowed from theoretical physics (often referred to as the 'many worlds hypothesis') that might have some utility in the context of our examination of narrative and *SimCity*. In this novel a decision has just been made as to whether or not the remaining aristocracy of Ankh-Morpork will raise a rebellion against the current civil authority (neatly falling into the category of those privileged historical 'moments' that we are so keen on isolating in our historical narratives) that will have a profound effect on the unfolding of the plot that follows:

> In a million universes, Lance-Constables Cuddy and Detritus didn't fall through the hole. In a million universes Vimes didn't find the pipes. (In one strange but theoretically possible universe the Watch House was redecorated in pastel colours by a freak whirlwind, which also repaired the door latch and did a few other odd jobs around the place.) In a million universes, the Watch failed.
>
> In a million universes, this was a very short book.[6]

In part this merely allows the whetting of the appetite of its readership for what follows through anachronistic reference that someone steeped in narratological theory would recognise as 'prolepsis' – the reader at this point will have no idea what 'hole', which 'pipes', or what might be exposed to the threat of 'failure'. Such proleptic foreshadowing is undoubtedly able to contribute to audience recognition of the well-told tale. This might be a comedy swords and sorcery novel, this declares, but this is a well-written comedy swords and sorcery novel, at least in terms of the care that has been taken over matters of structure. But it also points up a basic conceit of the fiction-making process, that the plot of the text is somehow uncertain until read, that we do not read to find out what is *written* next, but to find out what *happens* next. As Pratchett points out, there are a million possibilities unexplored, a million very short versions of this 'story'. But there is only one text held in our hands.

We put our trust in our authors to make the right choices among so many alternatives so that they will provide us with the most readerly pleasure.

All tales may be, as Nathaniel Hawthorne realised, 'twice told', but they do not often alter their events or emplotment when re-encountered in the same volume.[7] In a sense, it is even essential that they do not do so. Text, or at least the traditional realist literary text, has more or less been confined in its offering of a singular fixed version moving along fixed rails towards the buffers of closure. Literary academics might get excited by textual variations between editions, and the searching out of the smallest changes for their potential to invite new readings, but there is still a desire to end with an 'authorised' version. The possibility of the celebration of plural retellings is perhaps more evident in the case of film, where it manifests itself in the vogue now fuelled by the packing of extra material onto DVD releases of the 'Director's Cut' of various films.[8] But such deviations are more likely to be corrective in form – correcting errors of transcription, printer's errors, or the errors introduced by studio executives who had been paying more attention to audiences at test screenings than to the director of the film. All, however, end in a retreat into authoritative endorsement of a singular ending. And in that ending, in which justice is meted out (or not), virtue rewarded (or not), and the protagonists are orientated towards a 'happily ever after' (or not), we acquire a considerable proportion of the overarching meaning of the text, at least in respect of conventional popular fiction.

SimCity, however, offers something approaching the illusion of an apparently infinite possibility of potential readings. It has its constraints, and many of these are obvious – both in space (there are only so many diamond-shaped little boxes offered by the landscape grid on screen) and in type (you can only fill those boxes with certain structures, features or zones), but it pretends to a species of unlimited possibility. What Pratchett had borrowed from theoretical physics is the basic premise of the 'many worlds' hypothesis that seems to suggest that each 'decision' made in the world lived in (the 'datum universe') leads not to a closing down of what had, up until that point, been an almost infinite number of possible futures, but to the creation of an alternative or parallel universe in addition to that datum universe in which that alternative choice is 'really' enacted. We might experience our universe in terms of linear progression driven inexorably forward along a single fixed line, but all possibilities nevertheless 'happened' elsewhere. One reason that it is difficult to prove this hypothesis, of course, is that we have no access to such variant universes. As a writer of fiction, Pratchett tells us, he is not so limited – he has been able to select the most satisfying of the alternatives for the purposes of his texts. He can even tell us about the more absurd alternatives that he has 'discarded' before settling for a plot that is not only 'theoretically possible' but satisfyingly plausible. We are to be treated to all the readerly satisfaction of delayed disclosure (the finding of 'the pipes'), drama (someone is going to fall down 'a hole'), and tension preceding resolution (will Vimes 'fail' or not?)

SimCity goes further than this in presenting its own version of something akin to a playing out of the 'many worlds hypothesis'. There is no limit on the amount of the 'many worlds' that we might explore. There is no real hierarchy that establishes a single 'datum universe', except in fairly blunt terms. The manual for *SimCity 3000*, for example, recognises that the choices made by the reader might send us along the 'wrong' (or least satisfying) narrative line, particularly when disasters are confronted: 'Disasters happen all the time in the real world and SimCities are no exception. Before you unleash anything in your city, save the game.' In some ways this is analogous to hitting the 'quick-save' button before rounding a particularly suspicious corner in *Half-Life*, or backing up *Tomb Raider* before you send Lara Croft plummeting to her 'death' again and again as you try and judge a particularly irritating jump distance. Having spent many hours carefully constructing a city it is possible that the disaster you unleash might have similarly

terminal consequences for your Sims. But this is not a very satisfying analogy. In *Tomb Raider* you could sweep a particular level
clean of any obstacles and opponents and then wander around
looking at the game-world. But the play is over, and you are wandering around an empty stage. Once you have completed the particular plot fragment and Lara finally clings to that distant ledge
by her fingertips, or Freeman stands in a corridor now stacked
with alien corpses, the utility of the saved game is more or less
redundant.

The phrasing of the manual instructions has a wider ap-
plicability within *SimCity*, however. 'Before you unleash *anything*
in your city, save the game', we are told. In *Half-Life* or *Tomb Raider*
we save the game so that we can correct our failings of reading
when we fall into the error of in-game 'death' that will preclude the
possibility of continuing our linear progression through the game.
In *SimCity* you can save the game in order to explore alternatives
that are not so much 'correct' or 'incorrect', but are presented as
value-free. Want to switch the majority of your transport system
from road to rail? Save the game first. Want to rezone all that hous-
ing for low income families as dense industrial land? Save the game
first. Want to see what happens when an alien mother-ship drops
off a fleet of flying saucers? Save the game first. This certainly seems
to imply that there is no 'correct' course that we may identify. Making Sims use public transport might increase or decrease the growth
rate of your city, increasing industrial density may increase pollution while providing much needed revenue, but the authorial choice
of which might be most satisfying is handed over to the reader.
Even if the city is razed to the ground by alien invaders, the player
has not necessarily 'lost'. There is a potentially satisfying plot available in rebuilding your city from the rubble, of starting again and
laying out memorial parks in memory of those who went before,
just as there might be readerly satisfaction in watching your emergency services shrug off the effects of such devastation as they restore normality without any real pause.

What is of interest here is the way that the playing of *SimCity* provides so many possible narrative outcomes that do not fall into the binary opposition of 'correct' or 'incorrect' choice. The saved game of *SimCity* is not rendered immediately redundant, but can join all the other 'many worlds' that might have been, and we can do what the theoretical physicist cannot do, and explore that world at our leisure, making more choices and deviations that we may or may not want to explore further. We will still exercise ourselves in narrative terms as we approach successive choices, asking the basic question of 'What if?' that will then be worked out within the mechanics of the game, and we provide the 'meaning' of the plot fragment ourselves from our available conventional stories. Will this be the gallant story of recovery against all odds? Will my city thrive where the other cities of this Sim nation fall into recession? Will this be the tragedy of decline? Again and again we can ask the question 'What if?' as part of our engagement with text – we do not have to wait for moments of historical 'crisis' to present themselves. Everything here seems to point towards plural possibility, to a lack of fixity of outcome. The extent to which all this apparent freedom and supposed liberation might be illusory, however, will be the focus of the final section of this chapter.

SimCity limits

In some ways the basic framework of *SimCity*'s offer of limitless possibility would seem to invite positively 'utopian' readings. The term 'utopia', which has its origin in a coinage of Thomas More's for the title of his sixteenth-century political and philosophical tract, famously amalgamates the Greek words for both 'no-place' and 'good-place', which would appear to have a specific application to this form or game-fiction, just as 'half-life' or de Man's 'space between' proved useful in approaching earlier texts.[9] We certainly have been exposed to its inversion, the dystopian 'bad place' of the imagination, in both *Tomb Raider* and *Half-Life*. In terms of *SimCity* we are already aware that this is a textual construct, made of interrelated data fragments given graphical expression on screen, that is a 'no place', and the implication of the rhetoric of the manuals for *SimCity* is that most players are more interested in constructing the imagined 'good place' rather than any deliberately flawed or dysfunctional social construct. As such *SimCity* might be usefully thought of as a utopian text, at least in potential. Even when we encounter a contemporary urban problem such as traffic congestion, pollution, or high crime rates in *SimCity* we are unlikely to seek to preserve them simply for the 'realism' or verisimilitude they add to our fictional text. The drive is always essentially utopian, there is a demand for a movement away from the 'flawed' to the 'perfect' that we may or not heed that is always orientated towards finding something that gestures towards an absolute 'perfection'. The plot fragment then presents itself in the following terms: There is flaw. I identify flaw. I 'act'. There is no longer flaw. I move on until I identify the next flaw.[10]

Before embarking on an extended and hyperbolic discussion of the genre of the management game-fiction as revolutionary in offering us a point of access to a realisable utopian potential, however, the point should be made that it is the common usage of 'utopia' as popularly understood as a space in which a 'perfect' society can be imagined, rather than a full exploration of a complex philosophical idea realisable somehow 'within' game-fiction, that we are most concerned with here. The utopian ideal, that is likely to be something that no two players of *SimCity* would agree on in detail ('bigger?' or 'more efficient?', 'more profitable?' or 'happy?', etc.) powers the apparently absent plot of *SimCity* when it is played by what was described in Chapter 2 in relation to *Tomb Raider* as the 'conformist' reader. Specifically, this chapter assesses the extent to which the approach of any such 'perfection' in reading *SimCity* forces acceptance of a particular and singular world-view that is just as ideologically conservative as that which underlies the basic plot of *Half-Life*, and forces conformity where the promise had seemed to be of liberation from constraint. Perhaps we should always feel wary of any representative of authority (even the author of text, be they the writer of fiction or the designer of game-fictions) who promises and sanctions freedom, just as we should always be wary of those politicians whose offer to 'liberate' us only emphasises the control they already exercise over us, but the extent of its utopian potential might benefit from some consideration here.

SimCity is the longest established of the game-fiction series studied in detail in this volume, and it is perhaps appropriate that we can look to the reception of what has been described by some as the first realist novel in English, Daniel Defoe's *Robinson Crusoe*, for a degree of insight into how it functions as a readable text that has limits of convention that may be concealed, but nevertheless firmly structure the experience of reading. The sections of *Robinson Crusoe* that most casual readers remember is its central narrative of isolation, when Crusoe is shipwrecked on an island and has to pit himself against the elements and solitude with only his faith (and ship's stores, and books, and weapons) for comfort until he can add Friday to his list of 'goods'. Before he is joined by Friday and makes him his 'servant' Crusoe builds himself his own little kingdom from the available resources, making inventories of his possessions, keeping a diary, building and arranging his physical environment, and showing an attention to managerial detail that might be all-too recognisable to the readership of management game-fictions. Everything is focused on the transformation of 'wilderness' into 'civilisation', as he builds his fortress, organises his production of food and orders his calendar by cutting markers of the passing days into the trunks of the trees that surround his settlement.

This text initially presented itself as a 'true story' apparently grounded in not only the 'someone' of Crusoe but in an actual 'some-place', and whatever the sophistication claimed for contemporary readers, it is worth noting that many still regard the text as a 'fictionalisation' of the story of the shipwrecked Alexander Selkirk. Most critics, however, have identified a different and more complex relationship with the real in *Robinson Crusoe* than that location in simple autobiographical or biographical reference. This has never been a text read solely as 'about' one individual, whether that individual is defined as Defoe, Crusoe, or Selkirk, but as a text that says much about the cultural moment of its production – whether in terms of faith, individualism, or capitalism. When Karl Marx read *Robinson Crusoe*, for example, he was not taken in by the original conceit of the text, that it was a 'true' account of the shipwrecked Crusoe and showed the ways in which an individual survived the privations of shipwreck. Instead, and like all informed readers of his time, he recognised its fictionality. But even Marx, not primarily noted for the subtlety of his literary criticism, did not simply throw the text over his shoulder and turn back to a reading of Adam Smith's *The Wealth of Nations* because of his understanding that what he was confronted with was a fiction. Instead, he, and significant numbers of economists who followed in his footsteps, saw in Defoe's account a narrative that said something about the world we live in (or at least the world of emergent mercantile capitalism that Defoe lived in), and offered a reading of the text that stressed the extent to which it was not just a poor bedraggled sailor who was washed up on 'Crusoe's' island, but that entire economic system that has been described by Ian Watt as in Defoe's 'blood'.[11]

It is tempting to think of Crusoe's island as a tabula rasa or 'clean slate' on which Crusoe might create any utopian vision, just as the player or reader of *SimCity* is apparently able to create any kind of fictional version of society in the wilderness space provided at the moment of foundation of a city. This would, however, be a little naïve. Thinkers had long used such notions of an imagined space in a wilderness state in which there is as yet no social organisation for the entertainment of ideas about how we understand the social world we live in. Perhaps more significantly, many of the accounts of America's foundation and settlement also follow this basic model of understanding. But the insertion of human enquiry always makes this a certain kind of text, where we have already taken the answers we will find in the wilderness with us when we set out. We might not have the underlying systems of consumer capitalism 'in our blood' uncritically when we encounter *SimCity* as Crusoe has when he arrives on 'his' island, but we are aware that this 'sim nation' is modelled on the world in which we live, and has embedded within it the same assumptions and formulae through which social scientists have attempted to explain that world to us. We are already within a heavily and densely textualised space, even if it is apparently empty when first encountered. It already exists as text, and the invitation is to 'read' as much as to 'write'. In the welcoming opening gambit of the *SimCity 2000* manual we are offered an illusion of the 'unlimited cities' we might construct, but we are then presented with a further one hundred and thirty eight printed pages of text largely concerned with telling us what the rules that condition and limit that possibility are.

The bottom line that can never be forgotten in *SimCity* is budget control and fiscal probity. Indulge in too many utopian impulses and, unless you access the cheats and keep replenishing your 'simoleons', you will go bankrupt, your city will fall into decline, and you will 'fail'. Get deep enough into debt through bond issues and you can do nothing but watch your failure play itself out. Rather than the single 'no' of Lara Croft, we will be subject to a long line of petitioners complaining about where we have gone wrong. In particular, truly radical departures from the American model of consumer capitalism are simply not allowed for – the car remains king, you must go through a period of heavy industrial production which inevitably pollutes before you can concentrate on service industries or high-tech, low environmental impact industries, the skyscraper still offers the most desirable vision of appropriate land use, and there is a basic core progressivism that, despite the environmentalist concerns built into the game, drives the game ever onwards towards 'bigger', 'better', 'newer'. Even the regularity of the in-game grid and the top-down isometric vision of the world locate this kind of game-fiction in a particular context of how we read the visual image.[12] The cultural specificity of its 'American-ness' might not worry too many players in a world where our popular culture and mass entertainment constantly exposes us to American frameworks of understanding, but for a European reader there might still be a little regret that one cannot, for example, put in cycle lanes on *SimCity*'s roads, or put differential tax rates in place that sting the rich far harder than the poor.

It is not possible, even, to replay the mistakes of the command economies of the old Soviet Bloc in *SimCity*. A player cannot order one of his or her cities to produce only left footed shoes and another factory to produce (hopefully) matching right footed shoes, because he or she does not have direct control of the individual Sims, but only of general policy decisions. The player cannot restrict the movements of his or her Sims as the repressive regimes of the Soviet era did – if these citizens are faced with the digital equivalent of being forced to queue for too long, or to endure shortages of consumer goods, they will simply leave in disgust. The player cannot ration anything, or even use propaganda to persuade his or her Sims that the grass is actually greener, here, than it is in neighbouring states. Capitalism has not only won, it is the only possible model that might inform our playing of the game.

The basic method of control in *SimCity* allows us to set policy relating to a wide range of issues, but not to control the actions of the individual Sims who are presented to us as if they possessed autonomy. We can cajole and entreat our Sims to accept our design using a combination of carrot and stick, but we cannot directly order them. 'They' are given something approximating self-interest, just as the individual soldiers of *Close Combat* were given something approximating the illusion of self-preservation. But the artificial intelligence of the game does not allow us to appeal to the better instincts of the inhabitants of our potential utopia – the Sims are programmed to behave as if they are as concerned with a realisation of their 'self-evident' rights to 'Life, Liberty, and the pursuit of Happiness' guaranteed in a way that reflects current American understandings of what these terms mean.[13] The social contract we work within is the social contract of contemporary American capitalism. The extent of the coincidence of only a 'Sim America' as offering access to this utopian potential is even reflected in the language of the manual of *SimCity 3000*:

> [Y]ou're so much more than just their Mayor. You control their destinies. Sure, they can do some things on their own, but it's up to you to give them a nice place to live, to work, to raise their families, to pursue happiness, and all those other things they should be allowed to do. Just remember – if you don't give them what they're looking for, there's always some other Mayor out there who will and Sims can be quick to leave for greener pastures.

Inevitably, a 'successful' *SimCity* city will be an American city, and only America offers access to utopia, only Sim America offers 'perfection'. The basic offer of freedom of action or reading is tempered by our need to cater for these supposedly 'universal' desires, and if we do not conform to those desires, then we will suffer the consequences.

As a potentially didactic text that might claim to be teaching us something about the world 'as it really is', then, *SimCity* might well prove unpalatable to some. Despite the concession it makes to some rather New Age ideas about environmental issues (talking in terms of 'auras' as well as about material wealth, stressing that trees have more than commodity value) it is also grindingly progressive in its assumption of the valorisation of the 'bigger', the 'better', and the 'newer'. *SimCity 2000* is a little more blatant in making this clear, and declares in its manual that it 'is primarily a "building" game where you create and try to increase the size of your cities'. 'Bigger' really does equate with 'better' – size is important in this game. As time passes we get access to more and more technological possibilities. As the city grows in size we get treated to more 'rewards' in the form of civic buildings that might be useful or just reflect our stature as 'successful' mayors. When any aspect of the game falls into decline, we are faced with complaints and advice whether we solicit them or not. Even the cheat codes for *SimCity* communicate the extent to which the player is being asked to accept the values and judgements of a particular ideological system. In order to access a cheat that will enable purchases to be made with no cost (in Simoleons, at least), the player must access the command line and type in the phrase 'i am weak'.

That god games present us with the simultaneous promise of a liberty to do anything and the constraints of an imperative to conform (forcing us to accept what we must do to succeed) is obvious. In what amounts to an affectionate but satirical side-swipe at the genre Iain Banks had gestured towards the kinds of sim states that one can construct in the naming of a series of games in *Complicity*, one of very few novels in which a central protagonist is a player of computer games:

> *Despot* is a world-builder game from the HeadCrash Brothers, the same team that brought us *Brits*, *Raj* and *Reich*. It's their latest, biggest and best, it's Byzantinely complicated, baroquely beautiful, spectacularly immoral and utterly, utterly addictive.[14]

SimCity works as a game, and as a narrative, because we already know the story we are supposed to tell, already accept that the narrative reference made is not to the historical (as it was in *Close Combat*), but to the myth of American utopian futures. Banks uses '*Brits*', '*Raj*' and '*Reich*' to stand for something that is built into every aspect of the text of *SimCity* – a pre-existing narrative structure that we are then expected to conform to. At least *SimCity* does not attempt to use British imperialism and colonialism or Nazi militarism as its model, but however the expectations of the game are communicated, whether in its title or not, they establish limits above all else.

SimCity is not just a sim in the sense of truncated simulation, but a sim in the sense of simplification, for all its statistical complexity it is an abbreviation and reduction of the complex world about us. Some simplifications are barely noticeable – the absence of weather effects, for example – while others carry a series of implications that might be of more concern. Sims are a homogenous group. They do not have individuality and behave as a mass, even if we can zoom in and see individual animated Sims moving about the game-world. There is no racism, sexism or religious intolerance in *SimCity* because the differences between groups are either ignored or taken into account in a statistical model in such a way that everything is averaged out, everything is subject to generalisation. In other god games such as *Black & White*, however, something potentially more worrying is present.

The player can choose between 'good' and 'evil' in *Black & White*, just as you can choose to reverse the cover art and have a black or white CD case on your shelf, but you cannot evade the framework of meaning and judgement that accompany culturally specific understandings of what good and evil might mean. The punishment and reward system for training the avatar creature that moves about the game-world as your representative provides a case in point – the creature 'learns' by a system of reward (stroking) and punishment (beating) carried out by movement of a cursor that visually represents your godly hand. Anyone who has had responsibility for childcare will recognise the basic model, but the devil is in the detail. It is no longer socially acceptable to beat the recalcitrant child. It is indeed often, seen as an 'evil' act – an act of abuse of the child. And yet it is not an act interpreted by the game as having any moral value or as being subject to moral judgement. The player of *Black & White* might worry about the possibility of injury produced in excessive creature correction, but not about that act as an act of abuse. Behave in a fashion that is interpreted by the game's designers as evil and your actions will be written on the body of your landscape, and particularly on the temple complex raised in your honour by your worshippers. What can resemble the magic castle of Disneyland darkens and twists into spikes. But beating the creature is not so interpreted. One can imagine some grey areas not containable within the black and white moral system of *Black & White*, however. To sketch out a possible utilitarian problem, there might be moments of need for the whole of a settlement where the sacrifice of a few unfortunate individuals would serve the greater good. Whatever one thinks of the Benthamite notion of 'the greatest good for the greatest number of people' as a template for social behaviour and organisation, to label all sacrifice as necessarily 'evil' would seem to be extreme. *Black &White*, as its title implies, deals only in universal categories and does not allow grey areas. The vengeful God of the Old Testament, for example, would often be interpreted as evil by a system of in-game surveillance of the player that is implicitly applying the 'rules' of a Western European and North American system of values informed by Christianity's New Testament.

Such observation of an already culturally determined form of reading, however, should not lead us to reject such game-fictions because they have deceived us in the false promise of a truly open-ended experience. In that promise is one of the most interesting elements of the game-fiction's formal novelty and innovation – the multiple and plural is always prioritised over the singular as each plot fragment is encountered. There is something here that conveys the same kind of enthusiasm (and the inevitability of a collapse into its unattainability) as can be located in Buzz Lightyear's battle-cry of 'To infinity, and beyond'. We should not get too excited that the apparent absolute promise of the open-ended falls into a form of closure and ending, that this does not even approach the illusion of the infinite, let alone achieve the impossible and exceed it. In *SimCity*'s return to forms of closure, in our recognition in advance of future outcome, lies our ability to read this text, in its restrictive structure we are able to follow this as text. The game-fiction is open-ended within limits, open-ended for the moment, open-ended always with reference to an outcome (the building of our sim utopia in *SimCity*, the destruction of all other gods

in *Black & White*) that provide an implied ending that gives sense
to our readings within that moment.

Notes

1 Frank Kermode, *The Sense of an Ending: Studies in the Theory of Fiction* (Oxford and New York: Oxford University Press, 1966). Kermode's discussion of how endings operate in relation to literary narrative remains lucid and informative. His discussion of utopianism has also informed some of the more general thinking in this chapter, and the section 'Literary Fiction and Reality' is particularly relevant to my discussion here (pp. 127–52).

2 The one radical departure that Maxis have made from their successful formula emerged in the game *The Sims* (2000), which shifted the distance at which the player engages with the social construct. In *The Sims* it is the individual and the family that is subject to management, and the homes of individual sims that are the focus of the player's building activity. Much of what I have to say about *SimCity* remains applicable to *The Sims*, however. Visually *The Sims* remains more *Simpsons* than simulation, for example, and the apparent freedom to direct the 'lives' of individual Sims in any direction is comparably limited by a particular model of how social relationships work and career progression is achieved. The extent to which *SimCity* offers some of the pleasures of television soap opera, which I have not had enough space to explore in this chapter, are far more obvious in the voyeuristic observation of the everyday 'activities' of a small neighbourhood group in *The Sims*.

3 The clearest example of this would be *Black & White* (2001), a literal 'god game' in that the player is invited to adopt the role of a god who is worshipped, casts miracles, and uses a proxy 'creature' to guide his or her worshippers within a firmly structured and progressive story. *Black & White* was praised for both its story, its lack of strictures in how the player might approach the solution of specific tasks and problems, but was heavily criticised in its first incarnation for the 'micromanagement' its settlements required. *Black & White* will be given more detailed consideration towards the close of this chapter.

4 Unlike many games *Settlers* allows the player to watch the building

process, with assigned individuals carrying raw materials, laying bricks, and hammering planks together. Such construction work is far more detailed in its representation than in *SimCity* and provides an important part of the aesthetic quality of a game that nevertheless amounts to little more than a construction of a production line churning out soldiers, priests with offensive capability, and heavy weapons.

5 For a thumbnail definition of 'tech-tree' see the glossary of game-specific terms. It is worth adding, however, that the presence of such 'tech-trees' is another way in which game-fictions ensure that they conform to progressive expectations, much in the same way as the incremental access to the products of technological improvement does in *SimCity*.

6 Terry Pratchett, *Men at Arms* (London: Gollancz, 1993), pp. 21–2. Like Pratchett I would not pretend to competence with regard to the complexities of this thinking, and seek only to explore the ways in which popular culture has found something of interest in its broad framework and its relationship with forms of enquiry about narrative, rather than physical laws.

7 The classic example of plural endings, at least in literary fiction, is John Fowles's *The French Lieutenant's Woman* (Boston, MA: Little Brown, 1969). Much has been made of the implications of Fowles' instability of singular interpretation. See Linda Hutcheon, *Poetics of Postmodernism*, pp. 45–50.

8 The most obvious example would be the film *Blade Runner* (1982), where the restoration of cuts originally made at the studio's insistence, including a restoration of Ridley Scott's original ending and the removal of Deckard's narration (provided by Harrison Ford on original release), render the text far more slippery and ambiguous in its meanings. The inclusion of extra material on DVD release, including the frequent addition of 'the making of' mini-documentaries that reveal the artifice of the text might also relate to the discussion of audience appreciation of the 'well-turned phrase' that was discussed in Chapter 2.

9 For a more detailed discussion of both 'utopia' and 'utopianism' in relation to written forms of popular texts, see McCracken, *Pulp*, pp. 154–82.

10 I realise that I might have been able to call on the substantial support of a wealth of psychoanalytic theory if I substituted the term 'flaw'

with 'lack'. I wish to retain my focus here, however, on the way in which the reading of such a game-fiction is a self-reflexive process demanding recognition that we are constructing a textual artefact (a 'made thing', a 'text'), rather than answering a basic human desire.

11 Ian Watt, *The Rise of the Novel: Studies in Defoe, Richardson, and Fielding* (Harmondsworth: Penguin, 1957). Although the basic structure of this work owes something to Watt's volume, the relevant specific chapter in this context is '*Robinson Crusoe*, Individualism, and the Novel', pp. 62–92.

12 See Richard L. Gregory's 'Perspective' in Julia Thomas (ed.), *Reading Images* (Basingstoke: Palgrave, 2001), pp. 11–16 for a clear summary of the manner in which ways of seeing are not 'natural', but are culturally determined.

13 The phrase, of course, is from the text that in a sense 'wrote' modern America into existence (as a political state rather than a continental landmass), the Declaration of Independence of 4 July 1776.

14 Iain Banks, *Complicity* (London: Abacus, 1993), p. 51.

6   More than a game?

OUR SIMULATORS ARE NOT ARCADE OR COMPUTER
GAMES. Their cockpits and controls are identical to the real
aircraft, and they replicate the sensation of flying to extraordinary degrees of accuracy. **Participants should be 14 years of age
or over.** (Pamphlet advertising simulator 'flights', Yorkshire Flight
Centre, Knaresborough.)

Cyberpunk fiction and cyberculture theorising have no monopoly
of interest in the uncomfortable slippage that might accompany
the potential for simulation offered by computer games. The three-
way intersection between simulation, game and real, in particular,
has exercised different constituencies in different ways. For the Yorkshire Flight Centre attempting to drum up custom for their ex-
Royal Air Force F4 Phantom jet fighter simulator the stridency of
their objection to any possible confusion is communicated through
the use of emboldened block capitals. They really have a point they
want to make. The distinction between simulation and game
screams off the page – this is not a game. 'No children' this advertisement demands, or at least 'no children under 14 years of age'.
Simulation has 'participants', not 'players'. This is 'identical' to the
'real' they assert in a gesture towards absolutes, it 'replicates the
sensation' they admit as they throttle down through hyperbole to
be left only with 'extraordinary degrees of accuracy'. This might
not be 'only a game', and is therefore far more 'serious', and more
'adult', but it remains something 'extraordinary'. There is no prospect that this might reach an 'ordinary' degree of accuracy capable
of passing as the real that does not bring our attention, always, to
the exceptional nature of the simulatory event. This is not real, it is
simulation. As simulation it is not a game.

This lack of substance to any confusion between real, simulation and game is even more apparent to the player of computer games than it is to the customers of the Yorkshire Flight Centre. The complex and sophisticated flight sims for the PC might have now exceeded the level of visual detail available on machines once used to train combat pilots, but their players recognise that what they confront is realism and not real. It would be a rare individual player who would go beyond the purchase of a top of the range joystick and rudder peddles and invest not only in an accurate mock-up of a cockpit area but in the solid state hydraulics needed to replicate pitch and roll. Our PlayStation gamepads might tremble with their little internal motors when we fire our weapons, but this is hardly the kick of actual recoil. The computer game version of simulation is of a different order to those simulations intended to 'fool' as many of the senses as possible, and for far more practical purposes before they are sold on as vehicles for entertainment. For the flight sim aficionado the game is all about 'realism', all about 'authenticity', but with reference to the limits of the game rather than to the lack of limit of the real. Only the real is open to truly open-ended possibilities of action, only the real can address all our sensory input. The PC flight sim is the bastard child of the simulators used to train pilots, and does not make any comparable attempt to 'deceive'.

The player plays the game in the full knowledge that it is a game, and that life is not so conveniently organised according to the principles of narrative telling. The cockpit detail is present in our flight sims, but present on screen, rendered in something approximating three dimensions, but flat on the screen. We expect 'accuracy', but we do not expect or demand something indistinguishable from the real. We might have force-feedback joysticks, but few players have a set-up that judders and shakes when we hit air turbulence. Nor would many players want such a set-up, that would turn a diverting entertainment into something far less casual. Some gestures made to the artificiality of conventions of representation make sure that combat flight sims, in particular, remain playable as games, rather than attempt to confuse the sim experience with real experience. When flames run back from the nose of the plane we feel no heat; when we throw the plane into too tight a turn the screen might go blank to represent blackout at high-G, but we feel none of the pressure on our bodies, we experience no equivalent level of nausea. It is only a game – which is why we play. To play combat flight sims with the expectation that one might really die, or even be fooled for the moment that we might die, would severely limit its appeal. It would certainly take the 'fun' out of the experience.

All flight sims make greater or lesser claims to verisimilitude, with titles such as *Microsoft Flight Simulator 2002* at one possible extreme, and a pulp shoot-'em-up like *Crimson Skies* (2000) at the other. But even Microsoft have noticed that the addition of narrative potential adds something to a series that had often been praised for its technical sophistication but was generally viewed as overly worthy in its concentration on the technical simulation of flight. The 2002 edition of *Flight Simulator* might only provide fetch and carry 'missions' based around the kind of flights commercial pilots might conceivably be asked to undertake, rather than the barnstorming heroics of *Crimson Skies'* Zeppelin-busting and dogfighting against 'impossible' odds, but both are telling stories, rather than simply attempting to replicate or simulate the real. The use of the term 'simulation' helps to distinguish one title from another, and to describe the different kinds of pleasure that the specific examples offer, but it is always a term that needs to be understood in the context of the computer game, and is never a serious claim to a form of simulation that threatens our ability to distinguish between simulation and game, let alone simulation and real.

Not all reactions to this possibility of slippage between simulation, real and game are as stern as that of the Phantom jet simulator's owners, however. What might follow if we accept that we might no longer be able to distinguish between lived experience in the world and the fictional experience offered by the game-fiction has been treated with some levity, for example, by the writers of the British science fiction comedy television series *Red Dwarf* (1988–). Computer games in this far future have become not so much indistinguishable from life, but, as the title of the clearest example of a game played by the crew of *Red Dwarf* makes clear, 'better than life'. Of course, *Red Dwarf* is a comedy that veers between affectionate self-parody of that particular kind of masculinity that might be termed 'laddishness' and sending up the conventions of its own genre location, but in the process it demonstrates the ways in which concerns about the computer game as a technology of simulation are already easily recognisable to a popular audience.

The parallels that are drawn between the escapist fantasy of *Better Than Life* and the use of hard drugs also represent a clear nod to the cyberpunk aesthetic of William Gibson et al., with 'users', 'pushers', and 'game-heads' ruining their lives and presenting themselves as a social and individual evil that means that we should 'just say no' to the game.[1] A fairly serious satirical point is being made here, and the usual adolescent clichés of the computer game have been wheeled out as the deepest desires of the player's subconscious are tapped in a defensive move by the game to ensure its own survival. One of the crew members imagines a world in which his every whim is catered for by bare-breasted Valkyries; a sprawling multinational business empire emblematised by the presence of phallic 'Rimmer Towers' in major world capitals has been constructed by another; a third has engaged in mawkish sentimentality in recreating the milieu of Frank Capra's film *It's a Wonderful Life* (1946).[2] A joke is being played out here at the expense of many of the common assumptions that are made about the players of computer games – that they are male, immature, are only interested in women in terms of breast-size, and what they mean by 'better than life' shows the banality of an imagination stunted by the encounter with computer games rather than somehow nurtured

by it. The computer game as effective simulation becomes a vehicle for sixth-form pornography, for a classic compensation of
inadequacy in the real world, and for a sentimentalisation that even
the subject recognises as emotionally immature.

What is intriguing in the account offered by Rob Grant
and Doug Naylor, however, is the way in which they deal with the
issue of fictionality when the distinction between life and game is
realised by its players. Unlike Iain M. Banks's Culture citizens, the
players of *Red Dwarf*'s game should really be in no need of synthetic cues to remind them that what is represented is not real.
Players of *Better Than Life*, like the players of *Half-Life*, 'know' that
this is not the real, for all that the fulfilment of their inner desires
persuades them to lie to themselves and remain 'immersed'. *Red
Dwarf* is not merely science fiction, but science fiction parody, and
much entertainment is provided by the audience knowledge and
protagonist ignorance that this allows. The eventual realisation of
the fictionality of the experience of *Better Than Life* (and that it is
killing the players in the real world as they neglect all those inconvenient bodily matters not dealt with while we are playing a game)
does not lead to an immediate ending of engagement with the game,
however.[3] The possibility of immersion proves to be more than a
consequence of technical sophistication. The players stay 'in' the
game-world not because they have confused it with the real, but
because its very 'unreality' is attractive. This is a seductive, rather
than deceptive, fictional form. Only when *Better Than Life* ceases
to be 'better than life' do the crew decide to try and leave the game.

Instead of 'better than life' the player of the contemporary
game-fiction has access to something 'other than life', to textual
'half-life', to something emerging from a 'space between', to 'sim',
rather than 'simulation'. In short, they have access to text. Game-
fictions might be escapist, as so much fiction of various forms is,
but the utility of that escape demands our recognition of an imperative for return. The computer game does not allow us meaningful entry into another world any more than the Narnia novels

of C. S. Lewis (rather than the magical wardrobe) allow us entry into that world. Those of us who teach literature might be frustrated that we sometimes find it necessary to point out that Jane Eyre does not asphyxiate if we close the book, or that Hamlet (as character) is not able to make choices within *Hamlet* (as authored text), but it is not as necessary as some might think to make the same gesture to the player of game-fictions. We already 'know' that Lara Croft 'stars' in her own adventures, and that Freeman is both not us and not real. Rimmer might desire to stay 'in' his own management game while he is the success he has not been in life; the Cat might want to live out his puerile misogynist fantasy until his Valkyrie sex-slaves go on strike; Lister may prefer the sentimentality of Frank Capra's vision of idealised happy families to a real world in which he is the 'last man' condemned to solitude, but it is hard to see any game-fiction player or reader so succumbing to the illusion of immersion currently on offer in the games they actually play or the texts they actually read.

Realism is dead, long live realism

Whether or not the term postmodern is adequate to describe them, many of our contemporary works of fiction have obviously attempted to negotiate the demands of their moment of production and reflect cultural anxieties and cultural change. How we tell our stories to ourselves is as much a subject to debate as how technologies of communication might affect other areas of our lives. As J. G. Ballard noted when discussing the role of the (male) author confronted by the 'marriage of reason and nightmare that has dominated the 20th century' in a 1995 introduction to his novel of the city and the machine, *Crash* (1973):

> Can he, any longer make use of the techniques and perspectives of the traditional 19th century novel, with its linear narrative, its measured chronology, its consular characters grandly inhabiting their domains within an ample time and space? ... I feel

> myself that the writer's role, his authority and licence to act, have changed radically. I feel that, in a sense, the writer knows nothing any longer. He has no moral stance. He offers the reader the contents of his own head, a set of options and imaginative alternatives. His role is that of a scientist, whether on safari or in his laboratory, faced with an unknown terrain or subject. All he can do is to devise various hypotheses and test them against the facts.[4]

A possibly extreme reading of such a statement might imply that we finally have reached that moment at which the novel (or at least the realist novel that has been buried and exhumed on a number of previous occasions) is dead. Its devices are no longer adequate to the task of representation, and its techniques are disabled by the encounter with the present. The scientist, and not the writer, shall inherit the future. And yet Ballard's regret at the passing of authorial 'licence' and 'authority' should not be felt by the designers of the game-fiction, that product emerging from the very moment in which Ballard writes his new introduction to *Crash*. The break has not been so radical as Ballard supposes. On the one hand this sounds like a manifesto that could be adopted by gameplayers who foresee the ascendancy of the game-fiction, which is all about the testing of 'hypotheses', 'options' and 'imaginative alternatives', all about offering the 'contents' and not the authored and fixed 'meaning' of a single imaginative possibility. On the other hand, the game-fiction, as Chapters 4 and 5 should have made particularly clear, has not made the same kind of radical departure from nineteenth-century realism that Ballard sees as necessary for the writer of literary fiction. Game-fiction texts, as the brief discussion of *Black & White* indicated in Chapter 5, contain their own 'morality', allow us access (in *SimCity* and *The Sims*) to that same 'ample time and space' that had been the domain of a Dickens, a Thackeray or an Austen. Their imaginative alternatives consistently fall back into the linear narratives that reassure by their very familiarity, their characters remain 'grandly consular' in conception. The narrative game-fiction, still in its infancy but maturing rapidly, has not rejected its roots, but instead remains fixed in narrative traditions.

We can be so blinded by the sheen reflecting off our consoles and computers and by the hype of their public relations machines that we no longer see just how traditional the narratives on offer really are. We are always in danger of prioritising 'computer' over 'game', 'game' over 'fiction', and making too many assumptions about the 'virtual' that do not take proper account of the 'real'. The technological now that troubles Ballard as it appears to invert the traditional relations of author and text, real and imaginary, is also the focus of Jean Baudrilard's short essay 'Aesthetic Illusion and Virtual Reality'. In Baudrillard's words:

> We don't need digital gloves or a digital suit. As we are, we are moving around in a world as in a synthetic image. We have swallowed our microphones and headsets, producing intense interference effects, due to the short circuit of life and its technical diffusion. We have interiorised our own prosthetic image and become the professional showmen of our own lives.[5]

And yet in the encounter with the game-fiction all these trappings remain necessary. Baudrillard's conclusions, focused here on how we approach reality television, do not apply unproblematically to the computer game, and particularly to the computer game-fiction with narrative ambition or narrative purpose. The computer game is entertaining because it is extraordinary in content and form, because it never tries to normalise itself and simply reflect the mundanity of existence. If it did, quite bluntly, then it would be no fun. No fun, no reason for playing the game. It might still simulate, but it would not be a narrative text open to reading. The player of games does not exist outside of the world that Baudrillard describes, however. Instead he or she is always already aware of the act of swallowing the microphone and the headset, aware that he or she has entered into a particular form of reading contract with the text that Coleridge might still have been able to recognise. 'You don't bring my attention too often to the artificiality of this experience by providing inferior text,' it states 'and I will suspend my disbelief for the moment'. 'Tell me a story that I want to read,' our narrative game-fictions are told, 'and I will read on.' When we play the computer game we do not clamber into the cockpit of a physical simulator and accept that we are in a different and virtual world until the ride is over. Instead that contractual agreement is constantly renewed in an extended series of moments in which we exercise our willingness to be deceived.

One way of considering how that contractual agreement is arrived at might be thought of through consideration of 'interactivity'. Again, Iain Banks' gameplaying protagonist in *Complicity* provides a clear example of how this functions both in the present, and in a possible extrapolated future:

> Because *Despot* is interactive, *Despot* will go on building your world for you even if you leave it alone because it actually *watches* you; it learns your playing style, it knows you, it will try its little damnedest to *become* you. All world-builder games – emulating life or at least some aspect of it – develop and change according to their programmed rules if you leave them running alone, but *Despot* is the only one that with a bit of coaching will actually attempt to emulate *you*.[6]

To borrow a basic understanding of how we view objects from the work of Jacques Lacan, what we have here (at least *in potentia*, in *Despot* far more than in *SimCity*, apparently in *Black & White* and actually in *Despot*) is the object gazing back at us. It is watching us watching it. We do not simply 'look' or 'gaze' or 'watch' the unfolding text, but the text is watching us in way that can only have the potential to disturb in our age of increasing technological surveillance.[7] The essential characteristic of what is termed interactivity in relation to the computer game is that it *must* watch the reader. We act. It reacts. We act again. It reacts again. It rewards our attention with attention of its own. This might be presented to us in 'real-time' but we are locked in a complex dialogue or dance with the machine that amounts to a sequence of exchange that goes both ways. Even not to act is an act, and signifies. And in that dialogue of absence and action rests the fundamental claim to interactivity of the computer game. But this is also not simply a movement outside of history that debunks any common-sense misunderstanding of the act of reading as a passive experience in which the consumers consume like grazing cattle, but is intensely historical in a way that is distinct from our traditional understanding of the viewing of the object. The text we read watches us over time, it presents the illusion of 'knowing' us as we come to 'know' it, of 'reading' us as we 'read' it. The player of *Despot*, at least, is being textualised by the game, rendered into binary code that represents our action of reading in a way that means that our textual selves might be recorded, transmitted and replicated. We are not only given authorial responsibility by the interactive text, but we are becoming the textual subject.

How we feel about this, and whether our potential to all become something like Gibson's 'construct' Dixie Flatline, might mark us out as particular kinds of readers who embrace or reject the game-fiction, but it is going to be more or less inevitable as computer game-fictions increasingly read us as we read them. Such a move will not be undertaken so that the game-fiction might become a parasitic and dangerous text, as it was in *Better Than Life*, but so that we can engage in a joint act of cooperative narration that blurs the boundary between text and author in a way that would surprise even J. G. Ballard.

The shape of things to come

Matters of structural organisation inevitably contribute to meaning, and what might appear to have been an odd or even eccentric ordering of the chapters of this volume would probably benefit from some belated explanation. Faced with the task of looking in detail at four specific examples, the simple question of the order in which to place the individual readings comes to the fore. To fall back on the standard of chronological sequence (sequels aside, something like *SimCity, Tomb Raider, Close Combat, Half-Life*) would have made this one kind of text. Inherent in such an order would have been an informing faith in a kind of progressivism as absolute as that which is embedded in the operation of *SimCity*. 'Newer' would imply 'better'. We might look to the oldest example with nostalgia or historical interest, but not with any hope that it might represent the most advanced, or even 'best' example. To fall into such an ordering sequence would also imply at least tacit acceptance of the rampant technophilia that is evident in the pre-release publicity for computer games, in our relation to computer hardware, and in wider popular culture itself. Interest here, as in the spoof 'rockumentary' *This is Spinal Tap* (1984), is in the piece of equipment with the dial that goes up to eleven. 'Better' equates with an often disappointed promise of excess, with an impossible 'louder' in the case of *Spinal Tap*'s amplifier, and not with the quality of the sound produced. Or, in the case of such a privileging of the newest or latest computer game-fiction, better equates with faster artificial intelligence routines, bigger levels, higher frame-rates, more polygons, more on-screen movement, more account taken of more and more variables. Which does not necessarily mean 'better' game as narrative text or reading experience, only 'better' game as technical exercise.

The kind of games discussed in this study do not rely on our understanding of a newly instated digital or 'cyber' age in which things have changed, and changed utterly, but belong within traditions of narrative representation that go back to our earliest recorded tellings, and have been subject to critical analysis since Aristotle. When the need for the construction of a satisfying narrative is subordinated to the accommodation of increasing technological advance, then the designers of game-fictions might even be going down a blind alley, forgetting what it is that makes game-fictions readable and playable in the search for the elusive 'eleven' on the dial. The technology is a vital part of the game-fiction text, and of the experience of reading that text, but it is not the only element of the computer game, or necessarily the most significant, that we should pay attention to.

The second obvious option of ordering that was available was that based on the shifts in proximity to in-game events signalled through the placement of the point of view allowed to the player and the reader. This, in turn, would have implied that one extreme or another was more significant. Either the first-person camera of *Half-Life* or the near omniscience of *SimCity* would have been privileged. Either the god-game with its readerly pleasures of the illusion of the 'open-ended' and the possible, or the first-person shooter with its emphasis on the possibility of 'immersion' would have emerged, somehow, as victor. It was this latter possibility that concerned me most, with its accompanying realisation that it is an ill-considered misunderstanding of that immersive potential that has contributed so much to the popular unease that greets the game-fiction.

Even if we put aside the negative reading of such games as a contributory factor in school shootings or other acts of violence, then its increasing visual and aural refinement has taken our attention away from the thing itself, and towards the possibilities for future development it seems to lay claim to. The abstract is always given more attention than the real object. It is the first-person shooter, after all, that has had a mutually informing relationship with cyberpunk since Case first 'jacked in' to the 'matrix' in *Neuromancer*, that seems to offer a species of liberation (we can live in a hyper-real that is always more than the real can offer) and a species of possible threat (we neglect the real, and we die). To the Dixie flatline in Gibson's novel was given a surprisingly conservative attitude towards the potential of living a solely digital 'life'. The reward that he, or the construct that he has become, demands for services rendered is not the freedom to roam cyberspace, but the liberation of erasure. The matrix is certainly not 'better than life' for the flatline, but worse than 'death'. The point throughout this volume has been far more prosaic than Gibson's. Game-fictions might provide material for novelists and film-makers who produce truly startling works of enquiry on the unstable boundary between the 'real' and the 'virtual', but they do not, as yet, represent a movement towards the erasure of that boundary to any significant extent.

The final order in which the four textual studies have been presented here is an attempt to communicate variation without hierarchy, difference without ranking, and a recognition that game-fiction is a plural form in which a range of different strategic moves are made beneath the banner of realism. These are four readings of four very different texts, and the connections that can be made are not always sequential. *Tomb Raider* and *SimCity* offer more to their potentially subversive readers than *Half-Life*. *Close Combat* and *Half-Life* have a clearer relationship with each other than might at first appear, with both attempting to reflect the limits of possible action rather than allowing the superhuman exploits of Lara Croft or the 'godly' agency of *SimCity*. All these examples produce what we recognise as narrative, but they all construct that narrative in different ways and to different effect. If anything, in their variety and plurality they insist that we recognise that the game-fiction is a diverse cultural product, still emerging blinking into the light, but with the potential to develop into something significant as a form of narrative delivery that is currently restricted in its achievements not so much by the available technology, but by the creative input of its designers.

The computer game as fictional form revisited

How [playing computer games] affects lives
- don't have any other hobbies
- don't talk to others
- don't talk to families
- hurts their eyes
- don't get fresh air
- get unfit

- nothing else to talk about

(From 'How to Write a Journalistic Report: Writing Support Sheet' in a resource book for teachers, *Year 6 Non-fiction Writing*)[8]

I am not a social scientist, and am not qualified to engage in the debates that surround the empirical measurement of the amount of time spent (or 'wasted') in the playing of computer games by the young, or of the empirical relationship that may or may not exist between on-screen violence and violent acts in the world. Specialist or not, however, it is easy enough to identify examples of a negative reception of the computer game that demand some consideration even in a study that considers game-fiction with the same seriousness we take to our other forms of popular text. By chance I came across the above 'support sheet' for a 'writing frame' within a publication of resources designed for primary school teachers working within the English National Curriculum. Having read an example of a television report dealing with the censorship of films and the granting of certificates by the British Board of Film Classification, the students would be invited to write their own short television script within the frame provided on the subject of children and computer games. The accompanying support sheet is designed to nudge the student towards producing a certain kind of text. I have no quarrel with any of this, and would recognise the educational value of teaching our children to write for specific audiences and to be aware of the demands of different forms of writing.

The 'useful ideas' offered by the author of the resource pack, however, act as a thumbnail sketch of prevailing attitudes towards the computer game that might suggest that writing this book was a waste of time. Given the 'useful ideas' provided, the student is expected to engage in what for the player of computer games, even the player who would demand that they are 'only a game', would have to be an exercise in severe self-criticism. Playing the computer game is an asocial if not antisocial activity, it retards our ability to communicate, it ruins our family life, it does us physical harm, it leads to illness (and potentially, presumably, to death). It makes us 'unfit'. Other 'useful ideas' had invited the student to add that it costs a small fortune and fills all available time. It really does begin to look as if it is a social evil. Most of the negative characteristics mentioned in relation to the computer game might be made of hard-drug abuse, and the parallel, as with *Neuromancer* or *Red Dwarf*, is hard to ignore. The computer game appears to be a new opiate for the masses, a method of numbing the mind as effective as heroin or crack-cocaine abuse, and as disapproved of, if not actually illegal. As pointed out in Chapter 1, however, the same accusations can be levelled at the reading of novels, and particularly at the reading of novels with the intensity open only to the very young, as the sales of the 'Goosebumps' series of genre horror novels or the 'Discworld' series of comedy fantasy novels might indicate. That people want to play computer games, that they are potentially 'addictive' because they offer a form of pleasure not available elsewhere, is conspicuously absent from the text that the students are invited to write. The writing frame leaves them with nothing positive to say about an experience of popular culture that might have been a significant part of their maturation. As succeeding generations emerge unscathed from the experience of playing computer games without being transformed into gibbering idiots, attitudes might begin to change, but at present the computer game is the pariah of fictional forms. We should, perhaps, at least consider if it deserves such a dubious status.

Individual addiction or obsession is always an individual tragedy, but it is the extent to which all playing of computer games, all reading of game-fictions, is implicated here that is so extreme. As an educationalist working within the academic subject of English Studies I am aware that I teach literature not to construct a production line of future creative writers, or even because I have a love for my subject that I wish to share, but because 'reading' is a recognisable skill that is valued by employers and, even, still valued by wider society. And 'reading' in most university English departments has expanded its meaning beyond the study of a once fixed canon of 'great works' to include the reading of popular genre fictions, of films, and of television programmes. Although there might not be universal popular approval for such a move, we treat all such texts with the same degree of rigour, and with the same care as we treat the literary artwork. Whether or not at least that sub-set of computer games that I have termed game-fictions is similarly deserving of serious study needs to be considered if this volume is to come to a conclusion, rather than simply an ending.

There is something here, then, that might invite comprehension through the lens of Walter Benjamin's remarks in an essay that has often been read in relation to other forms of popular text, 'The Work of Art in the Age of Mechanical Reproduction'.[9] If the work of art of that mechanical age had been infinitely reproducible and homogenised, and stripped away of the mystery and 'aura' once associated with the original (that Cleanth Brooks would have recognised as the 'well-wrought urn'), then the work of art in our own supposedly digital age appears to restore the mystery and return the 'aura' to us – we all have access to, and only to, an original. The text I construct as I read *Tomb Raider* or *Half-Life* belongs only to me, and to me alone. In effect, 'I wrought the urn'. No other player or reader reads or writes the same text. It is unique. It is an original. Every one of us is author, every one of us is artist. There is something truly radical here, something significantly novel, something that demands that we rethink the ways in which we view the artwork, and our relationship with the individual work of art.

Until, that is, we boot the computer, insert the CD and confront the banality of what is currently realised within an intersection between text and technology that promises so much and delivers so little. I have no real doubt that at some point in the not too distant future we will see game-fictions that do move to break away from the mechanical to the virtual, and allow us to lose ourselves more easily in an immersive experience that will still have to have textual content to offer any appeal to its readership, but in the here and now of the moment of writing all one can do is look at the current crop of derivative, primitive examples and weep for what might have been and hope for what might be to come. *Tomb Raider*, *Half-Life*, *Close Combat* and *SimCity* are all pleasurable enough reading experiences, and were part of my own leisure time activities long before I decided to subject them to critical scrutiny, but I would hesitate to call them 'art' in a way that I would not when discussing the fiction of Iain Banks, even when he is writing genre science fiction with the extra 'M' inserted into his name.

Are game-fictions capable of being more than a game? Yes, as a form of fiction they demand careful critical scrutiny of how they communicate their meanings that might otherwise be disallowed, or at least never be undertaken, if we simply accept that they are a social evil from which our children must be protected. Are they 'better than life', do they even represent a threat to life? No, or at least no more so than our other fictions. As a form of fiction the game-fiction demands that it be 'read' and not simply 'experienced'. As the earliest cinema criticism recognised that film was a form of text only mobilised by the act of reading, and not something approximating the re-presentation of unmediated lived experience, so should criticism of the computer game-fiction recognise the act of reading that it demands.

Walter Benjamin identified the 'primary question' raised for the critic by an earlier technological advance as 'whether the very invention of photography had not transformed the entire nature of art'. At the risk of being another exponent of what Benjamin calls 'futile thought' (with reference to the blinkered critics who rarely went beyond questioning whether or not the photograph was 'art' at all), the same question seems to demand reply in relation to the game-fiction. As has probably become clear as we have looked at our series of concrete examples, the game-fiction has not changed the nature of art, but has presented itself as a novel experience of reading and telling in just as surprising a way as photography and cinema did before it. Whatever the future holds, we must do far more than 'just say no' to the computer game.

Notes

1 Even such a sympathetically presented game-playing protagonist as Cameron Colley in Iain Banks' *Complicity* reflects this fictional standard. Colley is an avid games player, a heavy smoker and a recreational drug user. By the close of the text he is diagnosed with lung cancer in another reworking of this direct connection between the playing of computer games, drug abuse, and the degeneration of the body.

2 References are to the novelisations of *Red Dwarf*, rather than to specific episodes where *Better Than Life* had been exploited more for the kind of dressing-up allowed by the presence of the holo-deck in *Star Trek: The Next Generation*. See Grant Naylor [Rob Grant and Doug Naylor], *The Red Dwarf Omnibus* (Harmondsworth: Penguin, 1992). *Better Than Life* is the title of the second volume (originally published in 1990), but the most significant section of the text in relation to the immersive potential of the computer game is to be found in the closing section of the first volume, pp. 255–98. (Both these volumes are included in the *Omnibus*.)

3 Computer games manufacturers address this perception of the danger of their product in a number of ways. The manuals now usually include sensible epilepsy warnings, but then go on to protect themselves with warning notices that imply the potential 'addictiveness' of their product. The inside front cover of the manual for the roleplaying game *Baldur's Gate: Tales of the Sword Coast* precedes all other matter with an extended 'Health Warning' that might be less condemnatory than some health warnings, but nevertheless looks like it belongs on the side of a cigarette packet. *Baldur's Gate* also uses the screens that load between levels to offer advice (rather like those irritating 'Tips of the Day' that can pop up when certain Windows programmes are opened) that includes an instruction to take regular breaks and to eat. A sceptical reader of such warnings might wonder whether they are not just providing legal cover against potential lawsuits, but trading on the implication of potential immersion through technical

sophistication that such warnings carry.

4 J. G. Ballard, *Crash* (London: Vintage, 1995).

5 Jean Baudrillard, 'Aesthetic Illusion and Virtual Reality' in *Reading Images*, ed. Thomas, pp. 198–206, p. 198.

6 Ian Banks, *Complicity*, p. 53. Emphasis in original.

7 See Jacques Lacan, *The Four Fundamental Concepts of Psychoanalysis*, trans. Alan Sheridan, (Harmondsworth: Penguin, 1979) pp. 67–79.

8 Sue Garnett, *Year 6 Non-Fiction Writing* (Preston: Topical Resources, 2002), p. 43.

9 Walter Benjamin, 'The Work of Art in the Age of Mechanical Reproduction' in *Illuminations*, trans. Zohn, pp. 211–44.

Glossary of game-specific terms

Artificial Intelligence (AI)   In terms of games, these are the coded routines that attempt to provide the illusion that the 'inhabitants' of the game landscape have an independent intelligence that is both unpredictable and conforms to a logic of context. A 'good' artificial intelligence routine does not just do the unexpected, but the player of the game should be able to recognise 'why'. It is related to artificial intelligence within computer science research, but its aim in the computer game is the satisfying *illusion* of the presence of another independent intelligence. Opposing AI that sufficiently emulates human intelligence to the point where it can consistently defeat a player would be unlikely to appeal to the players of computer games.

Bug   A mistake made in the coding of a computer game that results in a breakdown of in-game logic. Can be used to refer to errors that allow the player of a game to acquire 'unfair' advantage not intended by the game's designers. Can be frustrating, as the game fails to behave as expected, but can also allow the authorial constraints of the game's designers to be subverted. Useful bugs are often posted to Internet sites, while those that are simply programming errors are often fixed by 'patches' that must be loaded over the top of the original game.

Cheat   Not as damning a term as might at first seem, at least within the context of the computer game. Cheats are often left in a game's structure as a legacy of testing by the game's designers, and as an aid for reviewers who would not want to play a game through in conventional fashion. Frequently published to the Internet or in hobby magazines before the game is even available for retail sale, cheats can range in effect from changing any of the variables in a game, from the number and type of weapons available, to the degree of independent action taken by characters controlled by the computer AI.

Deformability   The possibility that one might effect the in-game environment in more ways than are purely necessary to progress through the game. Often considered to have a close relationship with the possibility of immersion, and usually used to describe the extent to which it is possible to damage or destroy areas of in-game landscape.

Easter Egg   So called with reference to the eggs hidden away by adults for children to find at Easter, these are related to secrets, but are necessarily deliberately hidden in the game landscape as rewards for proficiency of playing or reading. Does not always relate to a physical object to be found, but can be any deliberately concealed event, space or object.

Full-Motion Video (FMV)   An animated sequence, usually used to explain plot progression, during which the player moves from playing the game to watching the events unfolding on screen.

Immersion   The conceit that the player is 'in' the action. Most often referred to in the context of first-person games where the initial conceit is that what the protagonist sees is what the player sees on screen.

Isometric   A variation of a top-down view of the in-game landscape that presents some illusion of depth by allowing a view of three sides of objects. Such a view can often be rotated through the four major compass points.

Level   A term that has multiple usages in the context of the computer game, which indicates just how structured a form it can be. It might refer to the succession of individual confrontations that make up the body of the game, as in early arcade video games where one moved from level to level (or screen to screen) of increasing difficulty. It is more likely to be a reference to a large and distinct area that is geographically closed ('Venice' in *Tomb Raider II*, for example) or the equivalent to the 'floor' of a building. Depending on the game, increase or decrease in level indicates increasing difficulty of play. It can also refer to the progression of skills of a protagonist or other character, particularly within roleplaying games.

Point and Click   A method of interacting with the game that depends on moving a cursor over an object and then clicking a mouse button to activate information or response.

Real-time   The need for a continuing sequence of responses if the game is to take account of the presence of the player. A game running in real-time does not wait for player input in the manner of a traditional turn-based boardgame.

Secret   A difficult to access area or item that it is not essential to locate to further the progression of the game.

Tech-tree   A method of emulating technological advance within computer games, often by devoting resources to 'research' activity. Earlier advances (acquiring building technology, for example) open up further possible advances (such as sequentially more complex structures). Diagrammatically expressed, a technology-tree would resemble a family tree. The reliance on tech-trees in real-time strategy (RTS) and management sims reflect the frequency of use of progressive models of understanding for the basic underlying structures of computer games.

Top-down   A point of view that places the player at a fixed position as if gazing down on the landscape from above.

Walkthrough   A description in prose of the various actions a player must take in order to complete a level or a game. Often mechanistic (and lacking in any description of Easter Eggs or Secrets), they normally provide no more than instructions on how to progress further in plot terms.

Bibliography

Books and journals

Allen, Graham (2000), *Intertextuality*, London, Routledge.

Auerbach, Erich (1953), *Mimesis: The Representation of Reality in Western Literature*, Princeton, NJ, Princeton University Press.

Banks, Iain (1993), *Complicity*, London, Abacus.

Banks, Iain M. (2000), *Look to Windward*, London, Orbit.

Ballard, J. G. (1995), *Crash*, London, Vintage.

Barthes, Roland (1975), *S/Z*, trans. Richard Miller, New York, Hill and Wang.

Barthes, Roland (1972), *Mythologies*, trans. Annette Lavers, London, Paladin.

Barthes, Roland (1977), *Image–Music–Text*, trans. Stephen Heath, New York, Hill and Wang.

Barthes, Roland (1990), *The Pleasure of the Text*, trans. Richard Miller, Oxford, Blackwell.

Baudrillard, Jean (1985), 'The Ecstasy of Communication' in Hal Foster (ed.), *Postmodern Culture*, pp. 111–25.

Baudrillard, Jean (1985), 'The Precession of Simulacra' in Brian Wallis (ed.), *Art After Modernism: Rethinking Representation*, New York, New York Museum of Contemporary Art, pp. 253–82.

Baudrillard, Jean (1995), *The Gulf War Did Not Take Place*, trans. Paul Patton, Bloomington and Indianapolis, IN, Indiana University Press.

Baudrillard, Jean (2001), 'Aesthetic Illusion and Virtual Reality' in Julia Thomas (ed.), *Reading Images*, Basingstoke, Palgrave.

Belsey, Catherine (1980), *Critical Practice*, London, Methuen.

Benjamin, Walter (1970), *Illuminations: Essays and Reflections*, trans. Harry Zohn, London, Cape.

Berens, Kate and Geoff Howard (2001), *The Rough Guide to Videogaming*, London, Penguin.

Booth, Wayne (1961), *The Rhetoric of Fiction*, Harmondsworth, Penguin.

Carr, E. H. (1964), *What is History?*, Harmondsworth, Penguin.

Chatman, Seymour (1978), *Story and Discourse: Narrative Structure in Fiction and Film*, Ithaca, NY, Cornell University Press.

Cohan, Steven and Linda M. Shires (1988), *Telling Stories: A Theoretical Analysis of Narrative Fiction*, London, Routledge.

Cohn, Dorrit (1978), *Transparent Minds: Narrative Modes for Presenting Consciousness in Fiction*, Princeton, NJ, Princeton University Press.

Coleridge, Samuel Taylor (1983), *Biographia Literaria: Biographical Sketches of My Literary Life and Opinions*, in James Engell and W. Jackson Bate (eds), *Collected Writings of Samuel Taylor Coleridge VII*, Princeton, NJ, Princeton University Press.

Covey, Jon (ed.) (1996), *Fractal Dreams: New Media in Social Context*, London, Lawrence and Wishart.

De Man, Paul (1983), *Blindness and Insight: Essays in the Rhetoric of Contemporary Criticism*, London, Routledge.

Dick, Philip K. (1965), *The Man in the High Castle*, Harmondsworth, Penguin.

Docherty, Thomas (ed.) (1995), *Postmodernism: A Reader*, New York and London, Harvester.

Eco, Umberto (1987), *Travels in Hyperreality*, trans. William Weaver and Christine Leefeldt, London, Picador.

Ferguson, Niall (ed.) (1998), *Virtual History: Alternatives and Counterfactuals*, London, Basic Books.

Freud, Sigmund (1961), *Beyond the Pleasure Principle*, ed. James Strachey, New York, Norton.

Foster, Hal (ed.) (1985), *Postmodern Culture*, London, Pluto.

Fowles, John (1969), *The French Lieutenant's Woman*, Boston, MA, Little Brown.

Frye, Northrop (1957), *The Anatomy of Criticism: Four Essays*, Princeton, NJ, Princeton University Press.

Garnett, Sue (2002), *Year 6 Non Fiction Writing*, Preston, Topical Resources.

Genette, Gérard (1980), *Narrative Discourse: An Essay in Method*, trans. Jane E. Lewin, Ithaca, NY, Cornell University Press.

Genette, Gérard (1997), *Palimpsests: Literature in the Second Degree*, trans. Channa Newman and Claude Doubinsky, Lincoln, NE,

University of Nebraska Press.

Gibson, William (1984), *Neuromancer*, London, Gollancz.

Harris, Robert (1993), *Fatherland*, London, Arrow.

Hassan, Ihab (1982), *The Dismemberment of Orpheus: Towards a Post-modern Literature*, New York and Oxford, Oxford University Press.

Hassan, Ihab (1995), 'Towards a Concept of Postmodernism' in Thomas Docherty (ed.), *Postmodernism: A Reader*, pp. 146–56.

Hemingway, Ernest (1958), *In Our Time*, New York, Scribner.

Hemingway, Ernest (1977, first published 1929), *A Farewell to Arms*, London, Grafton.

Hutcheon, Linda (1988), *A Poetics of Postmodernism: History, Theory, Fiction*, London, Routledge.

Jameson, Fredric (1972), *The Prison House of Language: A Critical Account of Structuralism and Russian Formalism*, Princeton, NJ, Princeton University Press.

Jameson, Fredric (1981), *The Political Unconscious: Narrative as a Socially Symbolic Act*, Ithaca, NY, Cornell University Press.

Jameson, Fredric (1985), 'Postmodernism and Consumer Society' in Hal Foster (ed.) *Postmodern Culture*, pp. 111–25.

Jameson, Fredric (1991), *Postmodernism, or, The Cultural Logic of Late Capitalism*, London, Verso.

Kermode, Frank (1966), *The Sense of an Ending: Studies in the Theory of Fiction*, Oxford and New York, Oxford University Press.

LaCapra, Dominic (1983), *Rethinking Intellectual History: Texts, Contexts, Language*, Ithaca, NY, Cornell University Press.

LaCapra, Dominic, and Stephen L. Kaplan (eds.) (1983), *Modern European Intellectual History: Reappraisals and New Perspectives*, Ithaca, NY, Cornell University Press.

Lothe, Jakob (2000), *Narrative in Fiction and Film: An Introduction*, New York and Oxford, Oxford University Press.

McCracken, Scott (1998), *Pulp: Reading Popular Fiction*, Manchester, Manchester University Press.

Marwick, Arthur (1970), *The Nature of History*, London, Macmillan.

Malpas, Simon (ed.) (2001), *Postmodern Debates*, Basingstoke, Palgrave.

Naylor, Grant [Rob Grant and Doug Naylor] (1992), *The Red Dwarf Omnibus*, Harmondsworth, Penguin.

Poole, Steven (2000), *Trigger Happy: The Inner Life of Videogames*, London, Fourth Estate.

Pratchett, Terry (1993), *Men at Arms*, London, Gollancz.

Propp, Vladimir (1968), *Morphology of the Folk Tale*, trans. Laurence Scott, Austin, TX, University of Texas Press.

Rimmon-Kenan, Shlomith (1983), *Narrative Fiction: Contemporary Poetics*, London, Methuen.

Roberts, Adam (2000), *Science Fiction*, London, Routledge.

Robins, Kevin (1996), 'Cyberspace and the World We Live In', in Jon Covey (ed.), *Fractal Dreams*, London, Lawrence and Wishart.

Stallybrass, Julian (1993), 'Just Gaming: Allegory and Economy in Computer Games', *New Left Review* 198, pp. 83–106.

Suvin, Darko (1979), *Metamorphoses of Science Fiction: On the Poetics and History of a Literary Genre*, London and New Haven, CT, Yale University Press.

Thomas, Julia (ed.) (2001), *Reading Images*, Basingstoke, Palgrave.

Todorov, Tsvetlan (1977), *The Poetics of Prose*, Oxford, Blackwell.

Watt, Ian (1957), *The Rise of the Novel: Studies in Defoe, Richardson, and Fielding*, Harmondsworth, Penguin.

Waugh, Patricia (1984), *Metafiction: The Theory and Practice of Self-Conscious Fiction*, London, Methuen.

White, Hayden (1973), *Metahistory: The Historical Imagination in Nineteenth-Century Europe*, Baltimore, MD, Johns Hopkins University Press.

White, Hayden (1978), *Tropics of Discourse: Essays in Cultural Criticism*, London, Johns Hopkins University Press.

Young, Robert (ed.) (1981), *Untying the Text: A Post-Structuralist Reader*, Boston MA, Routledge.

Internet

Websites, particularly those run by non-professional organisations or individuals, are notoriously ephemeral. The official websites for the four major game-fictions dealt with in this work are given below, but use of a combination of title, developer and publisher in any reputable Internet search engine should call up relevant material. A useful summary work of reference that also adds something approaching short critical commentary to its listing of URLs is:

Rice, Simeon (2000), *Games*, London, The Good Web Guide.

URLs

Tomb Raider
www.eidosinteractive.co.uk/games/

Half-Life
www.valvesoftware.com/
www.sierrastudios.com/games/half-life/

Close Combat
www.ssionline.com/cc5/index.html

SimCity
http://simcity.ea.com/us/guide/

Games (selected)

Games are cited in the following fashion: *Game Title* (date), developer, publisher (in some instances developer and publisher are the same).

Age of Empires (1997), Ensemble, Microsoft.
Baldur's Gate (1998), BioWare, Black Isle.
Baldur's Gate: Tales of the Sword Coast (1999), BioWare, Interplay.
Baldur's Gate: Shadows of Amn (2000), Bioware, Interplay.
Black & White (2001), Lionhead, Electronic Arts.
Championship Manager: Season 01/02 (2001), Sports Interactive, Eidos.
Close Combat (1996), Microsoft.
Close Combat II: A Bridge Too Far (1997), Atomic, Microsoft.
Close Combat III: The Russian Front (1998), Atomic, Microsoft.
Close Combat IV: The Battle of the Bulge (1999), Atomic, SSI.
Close Combat: Invasion Normandy (2000), Atomic, SSI.
Command & Conquer: Tiberium Sun (1999), Westwood, Electronic Arts.
Crimson Skies (2000), Zipper Interactive, Microsoft.
Discworld Noir (1999), Perfect Entertainment, GT Interactive.
Doom (1993), id Software.
Ecco the Dolphin: Defender of the Future (2000), Appaloosa, Sega.
Gunman Chronicles (2000), Rewolf, Sierra.

Half-Life (1998), Valve, Sierra.

Half-Life: Opposing Force (1999), Gearbox, Sierra.

Half-Life: Blue Shift (2001), Gearbox, Sierra.

The Hobbit (1982), Beam, Melbourne House.

Indiana Jones and the Infernal Machine (1999), LucasArts.

Medal of Honor: Allied Assault (2002), 2015, Electronic Arts.

Quake II (1997), id Software.

Return to Castle Wolfenstein (2001), Gray Matter, Activision.

The Settlers III (1998), Blue Byte.

Shogun: Total War (2000), Creative Assembly, Electronic Arts.

Sid Meier's Alpha Centauri (1999), Firaxis, Electronic Arts.

Sid Meier's Civilization II (1996), Microprose.

SimCity (1989), Maxis, Brøderbund.

SimCity 2000 (1993), Maxis.

SimCity 3000 (1999), Maxis, Electronic Arts.

The Sims (2000), Maxis, Electronic Arts.

Street Fighter 3: Double Impact (2000), Capcom.

Sudden Strike (2000), CDV Software.

Tekken 3 (1998), Namco.

Tomb Raider (1996), Core Design, Eidos.

Tomb Raider II: The Dagger of Xian (1997), Core Design, Eidos.

Tomb Raider III: Adventures of Lara Croft (1998), Core Design, Eidos.

Tomb Raider: The Last Revelation (1999), Core Design, Eidos.

Tomb Raider: Chronicles (2000), Core Design, Eidos.

Unreal (1998), Epic, GT Interactive.

Wolfenstein 3D (1992), id Software, Apogee.

Index

Note: 'n.' after a page reference indicates the number of a note on that page. Page numbers in **bold** refer to entries given in the glossary of game-specific terms, pp. 157–9.